Sunspot Literary Journal

2023

Laine Cunningham / Editor, Publisher

Morrow Dowdle / Poetry Editor

Angel Leya / Graphic Designer

Rich Ehisen / Advisory Board Chair

Marion Grace Woolley / Advisory Board Member

Creativity is Power

Sunspot Literary Journal 2023
Volume 5 Issue 4
Creativity is Power

Published by Sun Dogs Creations
Changing the World One Book at a Time
Print ISBN: 978-1-951389-35-2
eBook ISBN: 978-1-951389-36-9

Cover Image *The Artichokes Bloom* by Matina Vossou
Cover Design by Angel Leya
Sunspot Logo by Timothy Boardman

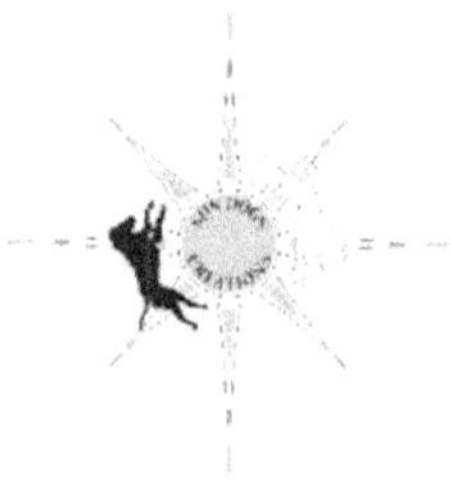

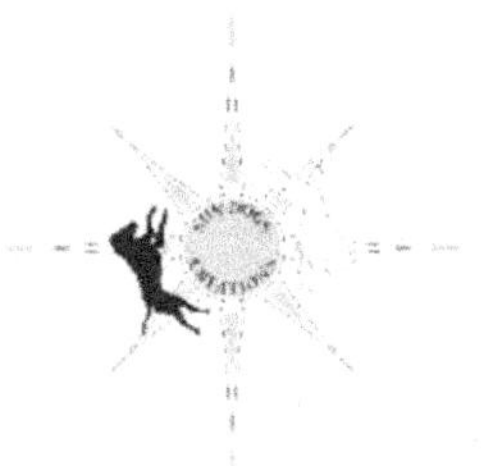

TABLE OF CONTENTS

Inception 2022

Goldilocks Zone 2022

Rigel 2023

Geminga 2023

Inception 2023

An Insect Floating

Carolina Esses

Translated from Spanish by Allison A. deFreese

Reprinted from the upcoming collection *Temporada de Invierno / Winter Season* with permission from Entre Ríos Books

An insect floating
sinking
vanishing in the water's murky depths.
With my tools I could remove the wings, its stinger,
but this one drowned
slid down the bucket's red rim
toward soapy water,
leaving us
age seven
with our thirst for dissection
intact
with our need to see
the loose pieces
of a horsefly
detach.

Un Insecto Flota

Carolina Esses

Un insecto flota.
Se hunde.
Desaparece en el fondo turbio del agua.
Mis instrumentos sirven para extirpar
alas, aguijón
pero éste se ahoga
resbala desde el borde rojo del balde
hacia el agua enjabonada
y nos deja
a los siete años
con nuestro afán de disección intacto
nuestras necesidad de ver las partes sueltas
desprendidas, de un tábano.

I Wanted to Rip

Carolina Esses

Translated from Spanish by Allison A. deFreese

Reprinted from the upcoming collection *Temporada de Invierno / Winter Season* with permission from Entre Ríos Books

I wanted to rip
a long winter from the forest,
to keep it inside me, to let it melt
like a splinter in my veins
so whenever I think of it
I turn into a wise old animal.
I went into winter as if getting tangled
in the stems of a blue-leafed plant
that only grows between stones.

Quise Arrancar del Bosque

Carolina Esses

Quise arrancar del bosque
una larga temporada de invierno,
guardarla dentro de mí, que se fuera deshaciendo
como una astilla a través de mis vasos sanguíneos
y que al recordarla
me convirtiera en un animal viejo y sabio.
Fui hacia el invierno, como si me enredara
en el tallo de una planta de hojas azules
que solo crece entre las piedras.

I'M NO GOOD AT GAUGING DISTANCES

CAROLINA ESSES

TRANSLATED FROM SPANISH BY ALLISON A. DEFREESE

Reprinted from the upcoming collection *Temporada de Invierno / Winter Season* with permission from Entre Ríos Books

I'M NO GOOD AT GAUGING DISTANCES
but I know the emptiness
between two stones
placed side-by-side
is the same void that opens between two cliffs.

The closest point between
us: our father.
Even so, I hear them say
these two don't have the same mother
nor share a religion.
Could we have been created from the same nature?

No Soy Hábil para Medir Distancias

Carolina Esses

No soy hábil para medir distancias
pero sé que entre dos piedras
colocadas una al lado de la otra
se abre el mismo abismo que entre dos acantilados.

La distancia más próxima entre nosotras
dos: el padre.
Aún así escucho que dicen
no comparten la madre
no son de la misma religión.
¿Acaso estamos hechas de la misma naturaleza?

LAMENT / BILL SCHULZ

DIGITAL EDITOR'S PRIZE

AFTER THE STORM / BILL SCHULZ

IN THE DESERT / BILL SCHULZ

THE END? / BILL SCHULZ

YOU COULD BE THE LAKE

Marcy Rae Henry

there are places in my house
i want to take you

afternoon light beaming in the center
of prosecco rings on my dresser

palm prints on the headboard
while the moon pulls us inside out

the lake eats everything
but not everything is digestible

you could be the lake
or you could be everything

something chest-level or top floor
or top shelf has me dumbstruck

water is a mystery
in all forms

you paused at my bookshelves
fingering orange spines

though not to scale, a tired map
contains the places we're from

i’m drawn to blue around the world
you move like a day across the week

one of us has to start
the other has to let go

POOL 2 / LIOR LOCHER

Blue Room

David Allen Sullivan

In its center a claw-
footed, blue-bottomed bathtub
seen through the slats strapped
around it for shipping. And what
he'd done in that blue room
was to leave it wrapped while he
shot thin shiver jets into his arm.

Sometimes warm, sometimes cold
but all he felt was hot ice entering
his body where he'd slapped
a vein awake, jabbed, and let it
take hold with a blanching shake.
He was coming awake. He was
dying for it. Catching a ride on
an outbound train that drained
what we knew of him.
We'd seen
him growing thin, and one by one
we peeled off, having said our piece
and feeling we'd said enough. Still,
he kept that same wild cackle
when he laughed, and the dopest
tunes. He'd pull off an earbud,
have me insert it, and we'd nod
together, skulls rubbing. *You're out*
following every finger, to still a doubt
but still it lingers, Jules Shear's high
pitched whine would fly.

Lee'd say:
This is the realest it gets. It stings
to remember. That blue tub never
got plumbed, he never immersed
his body in it. We washed him
after he was blue and cold. We
buried him with those earbuds in,
in that blue bathtub. Had to bend
him fetal to make him fit. Those thin
lips were twisted into a smile, as if
he was enjoying the thin joke of it.

To all my friends, if you're in need,
I'll leave my cell on and charged. Call.

Decay's Delights

David Allen Sullivan

Soil grows in me, blackens as it breaks down
what I feed it in the dark container of my belly.

It decomposes eggshells, splits avocado pits
in half so they tendril out feelingly, shreds

newspapers and blurs their ink until nothing
can be read in them save for blots. The buried bits,

grit of wine dregs, my first marriage, the metallic
tang of my addictions, are tumbled together

in my un-edited memoir's first draft. Fields I feed
the mulch to grow weeds with as much gusto

as spinach, latch crawls of squash, laddering vines
from which giant blackberries droop as they nod

and pulse in the least wind — am I a fool to argue
that weeds are the most beautiful? Ivy entwines

in our fences, pries apart mortar between bricks.
This rich, warm place in me takes apart as much

as it builds, asks only for my equanimity, my yes
to the everything it proposes. Growth and decay

are written on the crank handle. Turn it
over. Follow the worm trail. Freely spread

their castings. See what's gone to seed. What
comes back as something edible or beautiful—

or ugly as all get out, and every bit as worthy
as the stinky blown petals of this rose, browning.

Road Trip / Sheree Wood

THE FIELDS / SHEREE WOOD

After Night Rain

Valerie A. Smith

Dawn somewheres itself in the yard
between infant leaves and large gaps
of unfulfilled canopy, indulgent sky.

Overflow gonna flow, says the grey
that plans to stay all day, ash against
the grass turns pine bark purple.

New oak seedlings have fallen, soaked
to the wooden steps, a red stoop where I
had more than one talk with the Lord.

How long we've been here is marked
by a young man's death, growth spurts,
occupations. Redirection. We didn't love

the house, but we loved each other.
Pockets of rain pass over us with secrets
from previous places and times.

Tiger of the Air

Suzannah Watchorn

1 Wish I had the language, the hymnal voice you could understand, to sincerely proclaim my gratitude for the times you visited us, for choosing that tree at the top of our slope

2 as your perch. The first time I heard you I was in the attic, scribbling weepy words of despair in amethyst ink, asking God for forgiveness and more. Not faithful

3 enough, apparently, because I concluded you must just be a flock of sleepy pigeons. The next time, halfway downstairs, I turned and ran back up, woke up my lovely love;

4 in silence, we held hands, listening for you. He said you could only be an owl, swirling into stories of boyhood walks, Carolina parks, but still, I couldn't quite believe. So, I practiced

5 my version of devotionals: I started reading. You, my lord or lady, are a Great Horned Owl. You are secretive, stealthy, raptorial, *the tiger of the air*, your call low and long, four or five

6 hooting syllables. In the mornings those days, I questioned whether I could survive the winter, but those nights, with you outside, I flew through dreams of open wings, of tough, raking claws.

THE CROW / ALEX NODOPAKA

The Bagpipe's Tune

Jules Laforgue

Translated by Jefferey Samoray

No, no, my poor bagpipe,
Your lament is not so birdlike;
Nothing you say turns out right,
Pleases the ear or brings delight;

You see, Nature is the sort of spouse
Who crams ecstasy in our mouths,
And then, kills us, hardly polite,
The moment we pause to take respite.

Fine! She will do as she pleases,
Everything follows her own caprices!
As for us, we'll keep the nine Goddesses.
Kind muses of arts and sciences!

(Oh! Can't we just play some fine phrases,
To turn the tide, reverse the places,
So this mother so cruel and jealous
Would raise the thumb pressing upon us?)

AIR DE BINIOU

JULES LAFORGUE

Non, non, ma pauvre cornemuse,
Ta complainte est pas si oiseuse;
Et Tout est bien une méprise,
Et l'on peut la trouver mauvaise;

Et la Nature est une épouse
Qui nous carambole d'extases,
Et puis, nous occit, peu courtoise,
Dès qu'on se permet une pause.
Eh bien! qu'elle en prenne à son aise,
Et que tout fonctionne à sa guise!
Nous, nous entretiendrons les Muses.
Les neuf immortelles Glaneuses!

(Oh! pourrions-nous pas, par nos phrases,
Si bien lui retourner les choses,
Que cette marâtre jalouse
N'ait plus sur nos rentes de prise?)

Cloud

Jules Laforgue

Translated by Jefferey Samoray

Oh, let me alone, where my destiny lies,
I'm through with your false analogies!
Anyone upon close look would agree
That you, . . . you can't tell earth from sky.

Small proofs get on like scheming brothers,
Winking blue eyes less true than the blood flow
That lets them see: And so I go
Under a shady mask meant for another.

Ah! We're two sad killers baring our teeth!
Abused! Do you suppose this silly game
Will spin until the . . . How can I claim
To know when Time sends sword to sheath?

So; let's make peace, O furrowed brows! Drop your flint;
No staged regrets, bid the past good-bye,
Let's kiss the breeze while we wipe our eyes;
The night breeze, . . . her scent's a bit like mint.

Nuage

Jules Laforgue

Oh, laisse-moi tranquille, dans mon destin,
Avec tes comparaisons illégitimes!
Un examen plus serré ferait estime
Du moindre agent, . . . — toi, tu y perds ton latin.

Preuves s'entendant comme larrons en foire,
Clins d'yeux bleus pas plus sûrs que l'afflux de sang
Qui les envoya voir: me voilà passant
Pour un beau masque d'une inconstance noire.
Ah! que nous sommes donc deux pauvres bourreaux
Exploités! et sens-tu pas que ce manège
Mènera ses exploits tant que le . . . Que sais-je
N'aura pas rentré l'Infini au fourreau?

Là; faisons la paix, ô Sourcils! Prends ta mante;
Sans regrets apprêtés, ni scénarios vieux,
Allons baiser la brise essuyant nos yeux;
La brise, . . . elle sent ce soir un peu la menthe.

From the Facing It Together Series

/ Jack Bordnick

From the Facing It Together Series

/ Jack Bordnick

ORIGIN STORY

LEEANN OLIVIER

Eleven malevolent wolves silver
the dark, gifting gooseflesh, your radiant
bones croon, a changeling thing, a buckskin
blacktop zippered with stitches. David Byrne
sings sex and sin, sax and violins, still the world
keeps its spin. You wriggle out of the sundress

of your skin like a ribbonfish. Listen. A mess
of dresses rustles in your mother's attic, hems
hissing. In the pit of your chest a lock unclicks,
star whorls orbit in a glass carousel. Medics
circle your gurney, a pilgrimage, their
human ocean slaps and slithers, spilled

mercury squealing into milky bowls. The jut
of your wing bones knots indigo, rumbling
gulls gouge and purge, your tongue too swollen
to shut your mouth, your throat too swollen
to scream. You wrest your broken body from
this bed, clutching its jigsaw wounds, wearing

antlers instead of pearls, the ripples of a black
moon lapping. You're swathed in velvet
like a stingray, draped in orchid bulbs that daze
and bewile. Gravity fevers you through the wild
wood from maiden to crone, the second act
snuffed by rough male fingers, dragging

your jagged slander where the sweetgrass
and sourgum sandpaper your calves. Hoof
and paw, stalk and woodsmoke, a blight
of whitened sycamores, smokestack fumes
flicker and flail. You hunker in the makeshift
crawlspace, riddled with rot. Rain rattles

on the roof like a metal grate over a storefront
until urban memories dim, until all you are
is bristle and brim. Only witches live
in the woods. They thrum with want
and willow shiver. After the storm they
hush your howls. After the storm you are free.

How to Describe the Sky

LeeAnn Olivier

after James Baldwin, Jeff Buckley, and Gregory Alan Isakov — three kings of the Blues

Say it blues like a child playing hide-
and-seek in the chiffarobe after a hush silkens
the crawlspace, after a hush ices her blood

and she reckons *no one is coming*, her finger-
tips shivering along the furs. It blues
like morning glories, their white throats

unfurling in September. It blues like an electric
gecko hiding from collectors, her rare brood
slinking along the screwpines in Tanzania, ribboning

the forest with trills of turquoise. It blues
like a stillness that moves. It blues like a shining
honey-creeper, her birdsong a wet whip limning

the green. It blues like folds of Veronica's velvet
uncurling in the attic, food for grizzled skipper
moths, bluing their darting tongues. It blues

like moonstone, mystical, opalescent, a gleam so brutal
it breaks your heart and feasts on its ruby pieces.
It blues like a cobalt planet raining molten glass.

It blues like a sea anemone, tentacles lulling prey
to a rapture of lapis lazuli. It blues like the Mississippi
reclaiming her Orpheus, her kingdom for a kiss

upon his shoulder. It blues like broken bottles
glinting bright as stars. It blues like a triptych
in the Rothko Chapel, each canvas bleeding

darker as his oils saturate from sapphire to slate
and the artist recoils into madness. It blues
like a bruise. It blues like my father's eulogy, a daughter

and son expunged like a crime scene scrubbed clean. It blues
like the Caribbean cradling Buck Island, the way my love
and I dove from the boat to swim through it, a roiling

remedy stripping our maladies bare. It blues like a disease
and then it quickens like the cure for it. It blues
like music, like the only hue we've got in all this darkness.

WESTBOUND AND ROLLING / GINA MARANTO

Under the Skin / Gina Maranto

Aubade

Yakir Ben-Moshe

Translated by Dan Alter

Once a month the moon lowers its heavy eyelids, & sleeps.
One time a month, even that's too often.
I come to you carefully
in the gap between breath & breath's pounding,
in the gap between body & its substance—
someone scoops up your name:
half eyelid,
half drowse
treetops of stars make their way to the heart,
through which we thought to pulse toward the world—
my dear, where are you stepping off to at the moment morning
is kissing our moist dream?

שיר אהבה

Yakir Ben-Moshe

פַּעַם בְּחֹדֶשׁ מֵנִיחַ הַיָּרֵחַ אֶת עַפְעַפָּיו הַכְּבֵדִים, וְנִרְדָּם.
פַּעַם אַחַת בְּחֹדֶשׁ, גַּם זֶה יוֹתֵר מִדַּי.
אֲנִי בָּא אֵלַיִךְ בִּזְהִירוּת
בָּרֶוַח שֶׁבֵּין הַנְּשִׁימָה לְבֵין הַלְמוּת הַנְּשִׁימָה,
בָּרֶוַח שֶׁבֵּין הַגּוּף לְמַמָּשׁוּתוֹ –
מִישֶׁהוּ חוֹפֵן אֶת שְׁמֵךְ:
חֶצְיוֹ, עַפְעַף
חֶצְיוֹ, תְּנוּמָה
צַמְּרוֹת כּוֹכָבִים עוֹשׂוֹת דַּרְכָּן אֶל הַלֵּב
בַּעֲדוֹ חָשַׁבְנוּ לִפְעֹם אֶל הָעוֹלָם –
יַקִּירָתִי, לְאָן אַתְּ פּוֹסַעַת בָּרֶגַע בּוֹ הַבֹּקֶר
נוֹשֵׁק לַחֲלוֹמֵנוּ הָרָטֹב?

Synagogue 3 / Leslie Kerby

As You Drive the Columbia Plateau

Hardy Coleman

On this fortieth dawn of drought
          I have watched you sleep
soft as horses in clouds,
          jumping the wind.

Yet before summer's end,
          like a god of fertility,
you're leaving the Dust Bowl.

So I will find enough rope
          to snare the yearning
of these pregnant mares
          dissolving into birth,
dissolving in the thirst
          of this bone-dry continent you cross.

And I will mail you road maps
          of the dreamtime
a new home walks to.

And I will broadcast from the Teton Range
          everything that I can't tell you now.

And I will observe
        the flutter of your eyes this morning
as mine close every night
        until there is no night time,
no day, no setting sun.
        Until the years when there is nothing left
but a few cent's worth of wishes.

And I'll buy you a ticket to the rain.

Path to Lothlorien / Robert Palmer

Allegory of the Cave

Ezra Sun

the nest, bred of hushed
whispers. the moss, sprawling

from the body's edges. the lungs,
jammed in stalactite ash – pestilence of

each spored breath. & the distance. the
dusk. the warmth of touching lips.

i embalm myself in copper veins, simmering
into scabs. the reverie of a lie. a husk

bled of caustic dreams. & i dance, through
all five stages of my grief. my hands

play make-believe on shadow puppets &
candlelight projections. an eyeless

oedipus. the blind leading the
blind leading the blind.

A Sky Burial

Ezra Sun

Chiru cries mark contours of karst
jagged & torn. our hands cusp all
saṃsāra, unspooled & reknotted
by each thread. & i open: the river

is your mouth — a crescent arcing
in gnarled roots, grappled by both
its horns. the sun falls late & our

shadows sink deeper than soil. your
body surreal as a still-life, an
origami of earth. then it blurs:
sky to sea, sea to grass, flesh to

wind. mud-tar. coneflower. drums
tread to a hollow pace. in the end
nothing stays to reminisce.

DESTRUCTION / COLLEEN KAM SIU

BLOOM / COLLEEN KAM SIU

Rock-cut

Andrea Lewis

She can't do anything about the sunset – the daylight gone to waste, the darkened hills – or about copper extracted from the earth or sulfuric acid leaching through the soil. She doesn't love him, but she loves disruption. She wants to be the rock-cut the explosion leaves behind.

She can't stop children from crossing the border. Even now, they thread their way north, shoulders black against the sunset orange. She doesn't love him, but they park here by the darkened hills, windows open to the famished heat, the brazen air, defeated smell of dust.

She wants the hands that know explosives to know her. And to salvage anything that's left behind: vertebra, clavicle, metacarpal. She tastes the crevices of his neck and asks what chemicals leach through him or settle on his skin. He says: *You really want to know?* A rattlesnake of copper on his keychain drags across her thigh.

She can't do anything about the desert tortoise in its burrow, stunned and smothered in the shock waves. She can't protect the incubating eggs, the ancient line.

She can't stop the children from sleeping in the graveyard, where detonations rearrange the skeletons. *Ammonium nitrate,* he says. She doesn't love him, but she loves his downcast eyes, the narrow thumbs that graze her breasts, the knuckles skinned raw, his slow pulse. *And fuel oil. Nothing happens until you bring the two together.*

Now she rides the sunset, high above the darkened hills, above the pitted earth and ruined day. Above the final vein of copper-red before the night.

DISTURBANCES / CHRISTOPHER SQUIER

RHUBARB

RÓISÍN MCINTOSH

My husband is planting sweet eff all in the garden, but he lets on that it's rhubarb. Every morning, I peer out over the sink, ready to catch him as he stoops and kneels, chanting and invoking in the back garden. Thursday morning, I slip a sopping plate onto the dishrack and use my apron to wipe Fairy suds from my hands. I want to pounce, but he's up and striding to the tool shed, pulling out rakes, toeing at plastic plant pots, grabbing a fistful of compost. A war correspondent before he retired, he's never gardened in his life! This chanting is some voodoo, a darkness buried under our poplar and ash, cultivating in the dry muck.

More of his odd behavior. He spoke about the Juba witch doctors in South Sudan following that bit of bother he was in and the blood-black paste they smeared across his forehead in a smoke-filled tent outside the city. They were high on shared tobacco and fear, his jalabiya stained red. He'd cut his steak, reaching for the salt as he recounted how this voodoo man slowly cut the heart from a screaming fighter's chest and flung it into a fire before his eyes. Scooping a forkful of petit pois, he'd imparted that he was ordered to bury the ashes when they were finished, still hot and smelling of barbeque. He'd salted his potatoes and chewed, eyes fixed on the bare patch under the trees where the next day he would dig, having bought tools, a wheelbarrow, some crowns, and seeds, delving down with that blunt-as-bread spade. When I challenged him why rhubarb he'd paused and offered why not rhubarb, so I reminded him that as my husband he should know I don't like it, had never had a taste for the bitter stringy tendons disguised as palatable under a horror of sugar. He sighed that his mother prescribed rhubarb for constipation when he was a child, which is all well and good, but it disgusted me to hear him say it out loud.

When he absconded to Cape Town or the sweatshops of Mumbai or reported live from punk-infested Berlin or what have you, my home was orderly, and the children were raised as I liked. I didn't have to hear about constipation or make a man's dinner or starch his whites and separate out his darks. I could return to my lace coverlets, my unwrinkled cream linen pillowcases once the school bus had roared towards St. Gabriel's, leaving dishes to soak until half one with the receiver off the hook. The occasional Wednesday we could have fish and chips on my Royal Tara if I liked the idea. He only existed through hissing phone connections as the children took turns holding the receiver for infrequent calls that cut out just in time. On Sundays, the Joyces and Gilsenans would gush. How proud we must be of him, they'd paw, pushing past the children after Fr. Furey's eleven o'clock mass. That suited me fine. Then one evening he drops a beaten holdall on the front step, white-haired and retired mar dhea! Now he never leaves.

And this! When he's chanting on his knees I wonder if he is Buddhist; did they convert him in a Tibetan cell or was it when he interviewed the Dalai Lama that he got the notion to invoke Jesus? It turns my stomach to observe his paunch in the dirt, hands to the sky threading beads that he thinks I haven't seen, pathetic empty words on the wind. I'm just praying the next doors don't see him from the top bedroom, but I know how it is and they have. The next morning he's down at it again. I fly out, apron billowing, hands dripping wet, my house slippers sinking into the mud until I have him, and all the while the dead leaves whip round and the skeletal branches are soughing as they claw in the rising gust. I shout at him to tell me, tell me, what is this voodoo over the rhubarb, but tears hang in his throat as if to strangle him and he sobs in a voice no one has ever heard that it is penance.

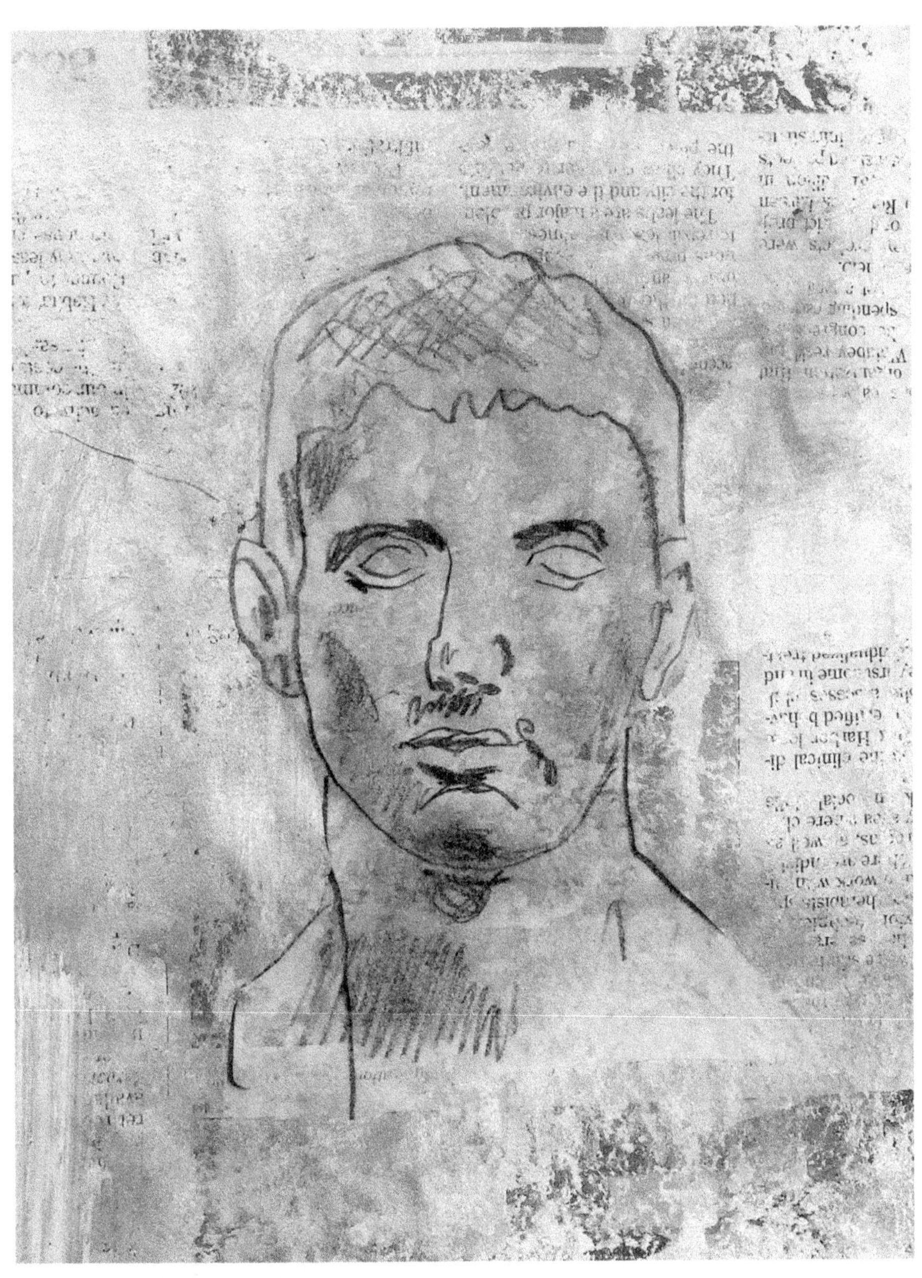

LION HEARTED MAN #3 / GJ GILLESPIE

Wonderskin

Myrth Killingsworth

You can visit my wound when the moon is full or when you have a lump of cedar in your pocket or the right amount of blue-spored mushroom in your gut or maybe in a fugue state (I haven't exactly figured out when, but there's a time) in the twilight, a time between, when the light shines as if through mist, but there's no mist, and it's late enough in the year, you can smell the bacteria in the soil, the air smells of rich rot and the spring bubbling up through horsetails. You'll know the tree because it will raise your hackles, lubricate your neck vertebrae, and sharpen your tongue. Face the tree. Squint through the half-light to see it. This slash. It is a yoni. That's a word for vagina. The one that doesn't meant sheath. And then. If all the universes are aligned and the stars and the earth, and the flora and the fauna of the forest and the microfauna and microflora in your gut, you can put the backs of your hands together. Make them into a spade, plunge them into the warm sap, spread the tree scar's labia, my artist's wound, and remove a grub. The grub is a queer assemblage. A wunderkammer of insect and animal and machine and dinosaur and maybe a baby witch. It is also just a grub. But big. The size of a human baby. Hold it like that. You won't know which end is its head but support some part of it. It will glow. Take it home. Let it sleep in your bed. Crack a window so that it gets fresh air. Feed it. It eats stories. It will grow big, and when it gets big enough, perhaps on the next equinox, or five full moons hence, or after three molts, it will ask you to eat it. But remember this: eating is becoming. Eat it anyway.

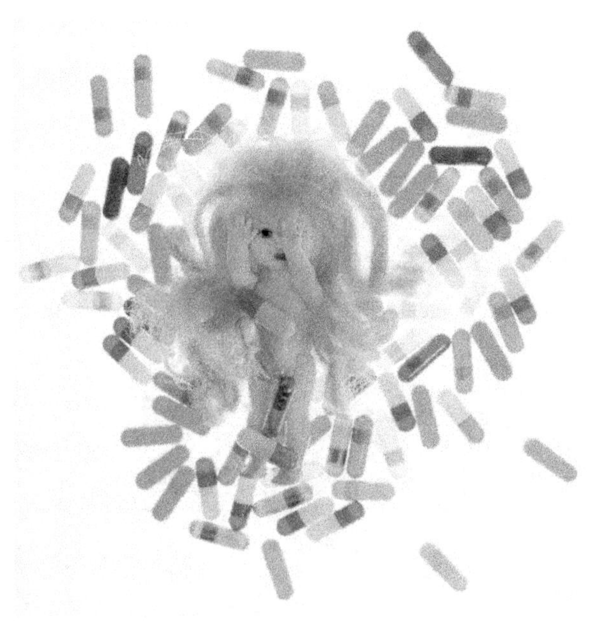

Too Much / Martha Clarkson

BRANCH / MARTHA CLARKSON

Glycerin: Starring You, Me, and Al Pachino

Yance Wyatt

I slam the door on you, since you slammed the picture of us on the nightstand facedown. The glass is shattered, so I stand it up again and think of how ironic or symbolic it would be if I cut my wrist with that glass, of how dead I would be, of how sad you would be that I was dead. Then I stagger back. So that's how it happens. It simply crosses your mind. Some of us just think it. Others actually do it. The only difference is, afterwards, you stand there like the people who didn't do it, only you're covered in unimaginary blood. I gather my wits, gather the shards and hold one to my wrist. Everyone cuts sideways, but that's not the way. That way, you just wind up sawing away at your tendon. But I'm bluffing. Bluffing myself, that's all. Hoping you'll come back for the last word and find me like this, and maybe that'll bring us closer. But you don't come back, and I don't have all night, so I get the dustpan and clean it up. Then I get in bed and put your pillow between my legs so my knees won't knock. I look at our picture before turning out the light.

The picture was taken on Halloween by whatshisname. We were the only ones not in costume, and somehow that seemed ironic or symbolic or something. You were hiding a half-smoked cigarette and I was hiding a drink. I can tell by the smoke slipping through your knuckles and the fact that my face looked sunburnt in October. Those were the days, right? Before you made me stop drinking and I made you stop smoking so I would stop smoking when I drank. That's when we started the movie marathons. We streamed all the new releases then moved on to the oeuvre of our favorite actors. First it was Hanks. We watched *The Money Pit* right after we moved in together, and when we watched *Castaway*, we promised to never give up on each other. Then it was De Niro, from *The Godfather* to *Analyze This* and *That*, though I think *The Godfather* may have been the beginning of our Pacino kick, or maybe the middle of Brando. Goddamn *The Godfather*. It made me want a glass of wine, so I drank a bottle. You had some too, which made you want a cigarette, so you smoked a pack. That's when we stopped streaming movies and started arguing again.

I think I'll go back to the bar for last call. Maybe that's where you went to cool off. If so, we'll get drunk and make up. If not, I'll get drunk and come home and you'll be here by then, asleep in our bed with that picture of us on your chest. And I'll kiss your eyelids, and fit my knees behind your knees, and smell into your smoky hair. I'll say "I'm sorry" and you'll say "He's not bleeding; it's just ketchup" or "She's not crying; it's just glycerine" or something else that doesn't make sense. But it'll make sense to you, won't it?

You slam the door on me, since I slammed the picture of us on the nightstand facedown. I drive eighty miles an hour and it isn't even the interstate. I'm trying to get a ticket, to get arrested, to get a whopper of a ticket so you can't afford to bail me out. I'm thinking about how easy it would be when you're going eighty to jerk the wheel a little and end everything. I'm thinking about the end and the beginning and nothing in between. I stop to buy some smokes but they're closed, so I bum one off a guy on the corner. He's nice enough, a little insane, and I kiss him on the cheek despite you, and he smiles with those mossy teeth then gives me another for the road. I light the second one from the first since the car socket is broken. Then I drive around our neighborhood looking into the dark houses lit by blue TVs.

I get home and you're gone. I brush my teeth and take off my clothes and find our picture there on the nightstand. You've been looking at it. I can see your thumbprint. Evidence of your guilt. But now *I* feel guilty.

In a minute I'll say my prayers, but I'll fall asleep in the process. I'll bet that's what it feels like when you die. Dying will be my last waking thought, so I'll probably dream about death. Maybe I'll have that dream I keep having, the one where I wake up with a horse head in my bed. Then my mind will fast-forward to the final scene, when Michael closes the door on Kay. And now I'll know I'm dreaming, so my conscience will yell cut, cut, cut, but I won't be able to wake up. To keep it from becoming a nightmare, I'll remind myself that it's all make believe: the blood, the tears, the whole damn thing. And when the cameras start rolling again, Pacino will become someone else. But it won't be Michael Corleone this time. It'll be you. Not your face or your voice or your name, necessarily. But it'll be you alright. I can always sense you there, a hovering presence, like a God or Godfather, reclaiming the life you left behind.

FIREWORKS / HARRY LEE JAMES

LITANY OF REMEMBRANCE

TAMAR JACOBS

We sat on a curb at the mouth of a farmer's market that was a little precious, a little boutique, not like the one in Baltimore under the expressway where we came with my first son when he was a baby, and it was cold, and I wasn't wearing a coat, and my father-in-law's new wife wrapped me in her shawl, and my father-in-law kept asking again the price of cabbage, angering the farmer, who looked exactly like an idea of a farmer, a big man with suspenders and broad calloused hands held out and up toward the sky in a kind of mime of emptiness, at-a-loss-ness, exasperation, at my father-in-law's repeating questions which read to him as badgering, bullying, harassment, not dementia, and in his confusion my father-in-law grew angry to match the farmer's anger and we walked away without any cabbage, my father-in-law's wife pulling me with her body in our shared shawl and her husband by his hand, back to the car where we got in and sat and waited for the heat to come on in the shadow of the jail where men stand in the windows at night and scream.

My son and I sat on a curb and shared a mango popsicle and a pint of pickled mushrooms. He took a photo of the mushrooms and texted it to his father, the son of my father-in-law, who is beginning to forget things, too, like his father, like his father's father I never knew, who my sons have never known. I thought the popsicle tasted just like a ripe mango, but for its having been pureed and frozen, and I wondered about the point of pureeing and freezing something that will taste at the end just like itself. My son said why aren't there any Black people here? Not even one like me. Not even a mixed one, is what he meant; I knew what he meant.

The phone vibrated in my pocket with my husband's response. I kept watching these people as the popsicle dripped into the clench of my son's hand and I did not offer my help, did not try to take it from him to get things under control, that classic transparent self-serving ice cream cone offer parents make angling for a taste.

I said, I guess it's the neighborhood. I said, let's find another one. I meant another market, but he thought I meant another popsicle. He thought I was ignoring what he said about the absence of Black people. Not another popsicle, I said, another market, and I told him about the one under the bridge in Baltimore. I didn't tell him about his grandfather and the cabbage. I tell him all the time, he and his brother, about their people who are gone. We remember them. We remember them. In all seasons we remember them. This is the Jewish Litany of Remembrance that I love. I sanitize the stories sometimes, embellish them sometimes, and tell myself I'll pare them back later to what's real as if the truth were a banana and words were the peel.

I didn't tell him about the cabbage, and I didn't tell him about the strip club in the shadow of the jail in Baltimore where a stripper stopped and looked at a group of us off our shared shift, then squatted, penis in hand, stroking it as we tried to chat with him, chat over this thing he was doing — we were embarrassed, this was too much even though wasn't it what we'd come for? We'd walked into that place, that club not far from that market, in the shadow of the jail where men would stand at the cracked windows and scream, but in the mornings I don't remember them yelling so much as they did in the nights and I remember now, on the curb with our melting mango sorbet and mushrooms, number 17 on the questionnaire from the neurologist asking if the patient is showing signs of increasing disturbances at night. Sundowning, this is what the question is headed toward. No, not yet.

I didn't answer my son, really, but addressed the thing after where the answer should have been. Let's find another one, I said. I handed my child the phone and he smiled to read his father's response: a wordless screen full of mushrooms and heart emojis just for him, a perfect response from my husband who is beginning to forget, like the mango popsicle was soon forgotten, a spot of orange on the ground perfectly round as the sun high over us before it seems like it begins to fall but is really sitting still, our star, as we spin off into the dark.

How our babies used to scream. How babies scream. This is their defining thing, the screaming, because they can't be understood. Like the men in the windows at the jail aim their voices out at anyone on the other side, trying to voice with their noise the frustrations of their repeating world. I remember them. I remember them. In all seasons, I do.

Barbeque

Tamar Jacobs

I wanted to make him happy, so I told him I'd barbeque. While he was at school, I went and bought pig meat forced into tubes and a bag of charcoal and I bought four patties of beef flesh ground and patted down into discs. I lit a fire and laid these things on it until the discs of beef flesh darkened and contracted, until the entubed pig meat blistered and began to blacken

and then I took all this off the fire and called my son down from where he was holding his eyes on a screen watching videos conceived and directed by a man whose voice pipes in at the end to hammer home his morals, to heavy hand them in case anyone's missed the message. He says, "So you see . . ." and you wait for it, it's in that sentence, the whole point of what you've just seen. The universal takeaway. Like Aesop, the form. They run one after the next, these videos, and my son sits and watches them, docile and accepting of the reel, whatever comes next, whatever the message the voice at the end will ask him to swallow.

We ate everything: he did, and I did, too. I was hungry, and the bread was soft, and I remembered times I've eaten those things, looked forward to eating things like those. We finished quickly. He ate fast, in huge, uncomfortable looking bites, he'd been hungry, and while we ate I ignored my phone pinging texts at me I knew was text thread of our neighbors' grievances about how the playground on our corner is out of control now, preteens unsupervised and cursing, with nowhere to go now that school's out. I've heard

that when a pig is afraid it screams like a human. I've heard cows have distinct adolescences, moody and prone to actions which might seem rash, nonsensical. My son sat and chewed, his back facing me, looking out into our yard, up into the trees beyond it. He was quiet and I was quiet, too. I wanted to make him happy.

Now We Can Move Forward

Tamar Jacobs

She asked, politely, *how is your husband*, and I paused, said, well . . . and watched her get ready for whatever comes after a pause like that. I imagined a list of things she might be bracing for: separation, affairs, depression, then I erased the possibility of them with my response, and she said, *but he's so young*, and I told her all the things in all the brains running through his family, a funny word, *running*, like a leak, like to flee, like to make fast progress forward, and her face stayed placid, I thought, strangely so, though then she said what you'd expect, *I'm so sorry*. I tried to backpedal the awkward thing on us now, as we trailed our children around this windowless warehouse of an arcade, not too close but also not so far we might lose them; they are the age now when they want to be able to feel they don't need you even as you are near, just beyond their sight, enabling this trick of their own perception, and I tried to say some version of, *it was hard at first but now it's better, really, it's a relief, now we can move forward*. The words felt like chalk in my mouth because the first time I said them, they were true, but with each successive time I speak them, they are composed of higher concentrations of performance, smelling like the need for the words to accomplish something, as with memories, how the more times you reach for them, to feel the feelings you feel when you reach for them, they are less from the fabric of the actual remembered moment, maybe even nothing at all, maybe full fiction at a point, full creation for the purpose of feeling escape from a new moment you might choose to remember differently later. Her face was so placid, I thought, as I paid for an hour of ping pong, from our waning pool of money, its own form of willful pretending, how I insisted on paying for all of us, and we watched our sons and said the things you say to a person who isn't quite your own friend, about your two sons playing ping pong before you, like how tall they've grown in the time since you were last together and how many boxes of cereal they eat in a day and can you believe that, it's astonishing. But what else could there be? Wasn't she following the laws of conversation by volleying back my own tone? My own strange calm delivery of the news my husband had lost one, then a second job, because they've noticed he forgets? That his forgetting has progressed? *I'm relieved*, I'd said to her. And what did I want her to say to this strange thing? I'm not relieved, no, that's not the word for what I am.

After ping pong we sat and ate in a food court, and here our sons began to try to outburp one another, and my son lapped with his tongue at his little parcel of BBQ sauce like a kitten, said, oh, this is *delicious*, and all four of us laughed, and our sons continued with this behavior even though we told them to stop, because we were still laughing, because they knew what our laughter meant, it meant what we were saying was not true, it didn't match our words, the laughter did not, and the thing to listen for was our laughter, which would reveal the truth of the mood of the thing happening and the trouble, I thought, I think, is there isn't always laughter to follow, to figure from and I wish I could ignore what's true, lick up my barbeque sauce the way you aren't supposed to.

COVID COLOR O / CYNTHIA YATCHMAN

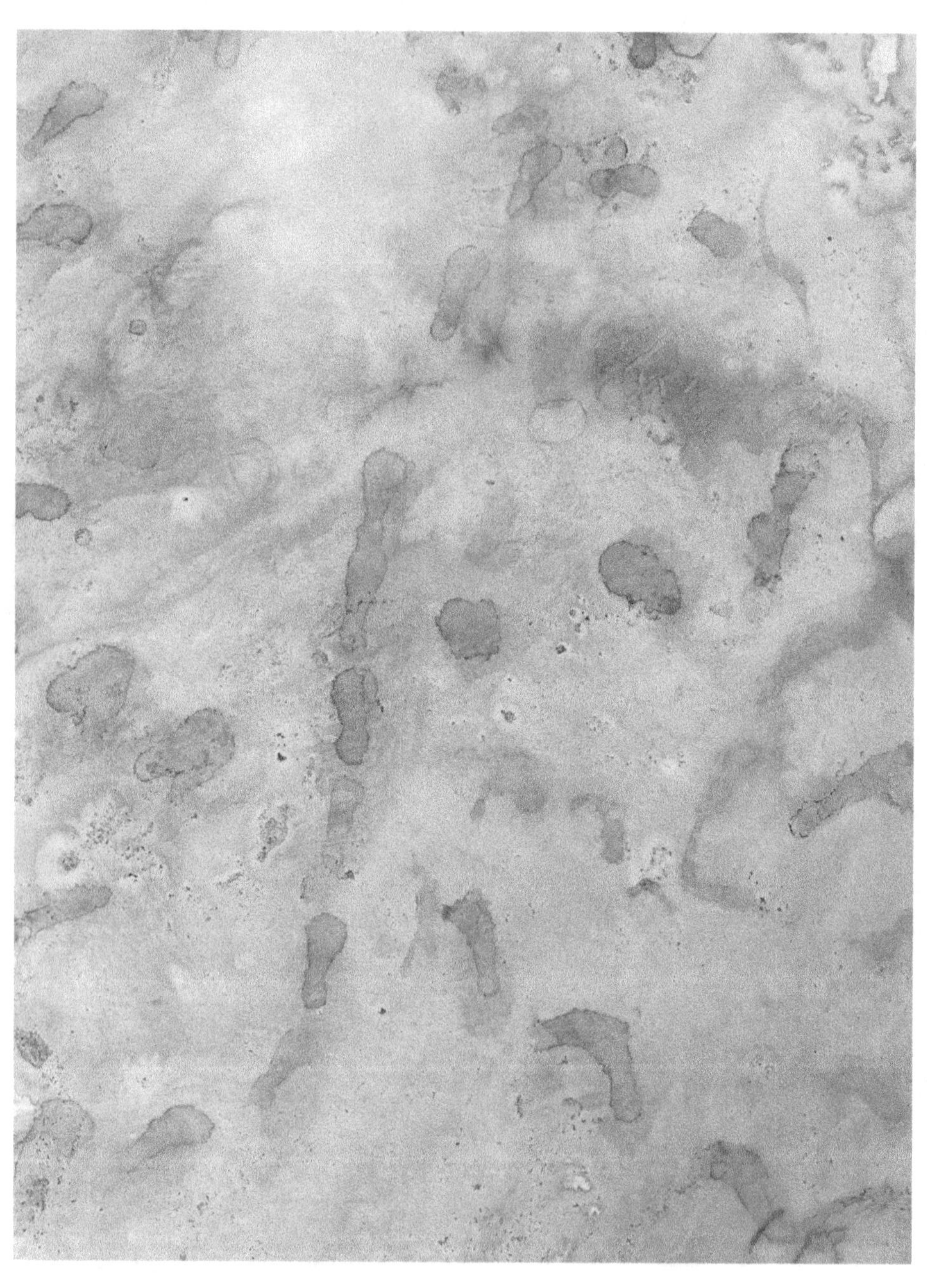

COVID COLOR 2022 GG / CYNTHIA YATCHMAN

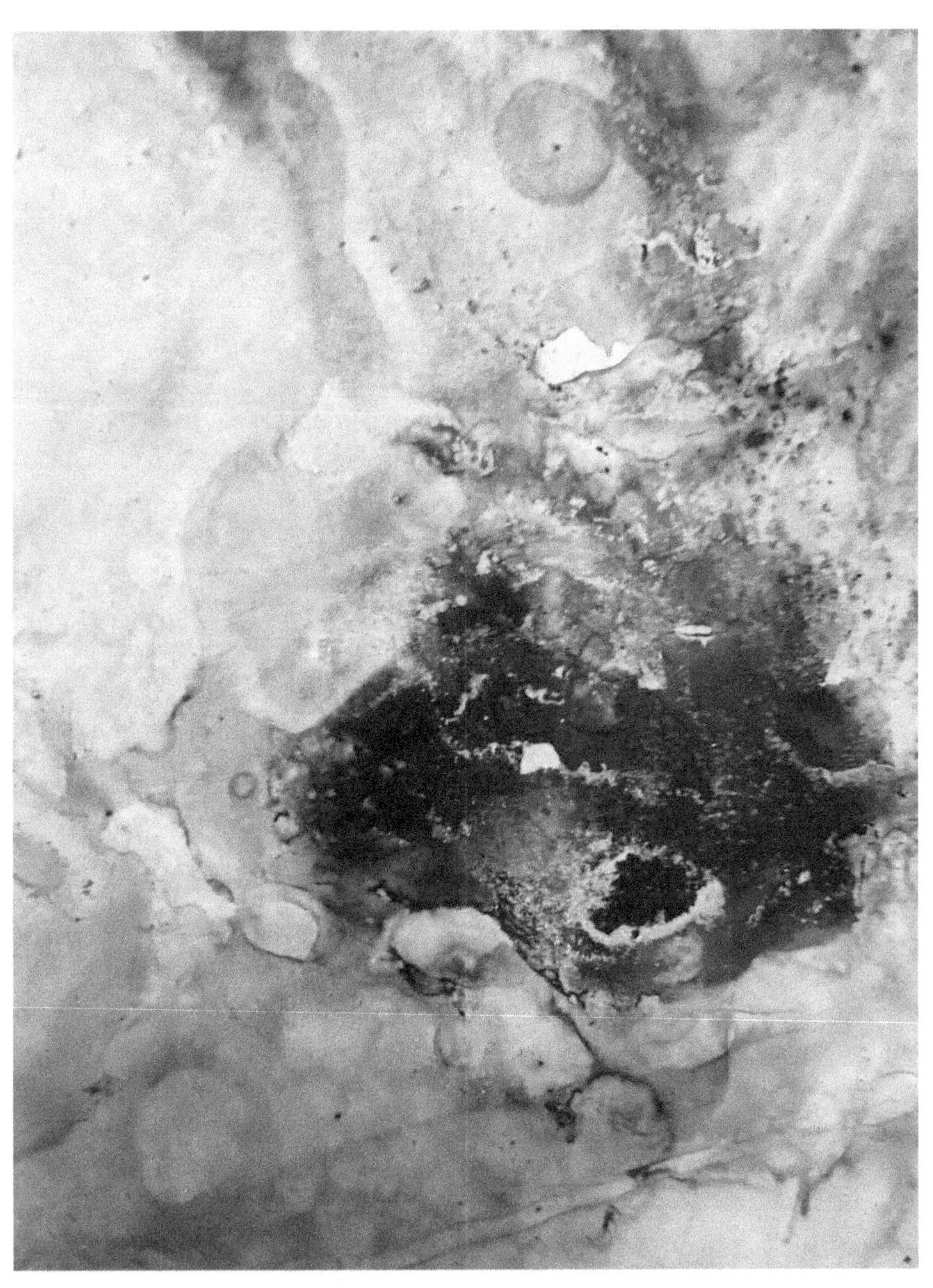

COVID COLOR 2022 H / CYNTHIA YATCHMAN

Cold Spring

Michael Murphy

Bo would rather be throwing rocks at cars. Hidden behind the curtain of kudzu that hangs at the bend in the road. Where Brother Eli smokes and tied that neighbor girl to a tree. Where Poppa Wheelie will become Poppa Wheelie.

Not today. Momma's having a spell and the haven of that in-between space is miles away. He's on a short leash — it's been a week since he asked what *nigger* meant and Daddy-Jim grew legs.

The bathroom is second best. When he turns the lock on the door, no one in the world knows where he is. It's a windowless nowhere — all cool tile and bleachy clean.

Momma leans her head against the wall phone. Twirls the cord around her fingers and says, "He's just a boy." As Bo makes for the bathroom, she spasms. One hand white-knuckles the receiver, the other rises open-palmed. Swinging down, she's yanked back by the cord like a dog chained to a tree. There's no getting past her. She's smiling like the devil.

Surrendering, Bo sits outside — Indian-style, in the cold. It's a contortion that makes Brother Eli cringe. "You're gonna get stuck that way," he'll spit, before heading this way or that.

The backyard isn't much but rides high. From his perch, he can see forever; down through the pines, across Morrow's field to the duck pond. They're like a storybook — momma duck, baby duck, baby duck. They don't belong here. Smuggled into town in the back of the neighbor's station wagon.

Bo was somewhere else last year. Before then, somewhere else. He slowly scans from ridge to ridge. In this place, at this time, his world is thirty seconds across. "A bunch of nuthin'." The words are Momma's. As they leave his mouth, they're eaten by the pines.

In the middle of those ridges — on the far, grassy rise behind the pond — is the water tower. Even from here you can read *Pinnacle* painted bold and black. "In case y'ever forget where you are."

A copper cushion of pine needles blankets the yard from porch to field. It keeps things clean and quiet. Pine needles make good kindling. Pine will take a flame. It will burn fast and hot. It will snap and pop and smoke like hell. The smell of it hangs thick in the air. It's March and the winter wood is gone.

The smell of chimneys, a windy chill, and the lonesome song of the whip-poor-will, reads the last page of Momma's diary. Bo closes his eyes and mutely mouths the words.

Near the neighbors' place, three dogwoods grow around the green box. There was a hint of heat last week that cheated white flowers out of them. The duck lady next door would lie on the box and stare — drinking Mountain Dew from the bottle with a silly straw. The box is always warm. Her fat arms and legs melt over its sides. Daddy-Jim's electric box. *My money keeps that hummin', boy.*

Always humming, always warm, always there — Bo wakes and falls asleep to it. In his dreams, it rumbles like a rocket ship, mumbles like ghosts. Awake, it's old men praying, sad and sorry for some grownup sin.

—Follow me—

Bo opens his eyes.

—Follow me—

—Follow me, me, me—

—Follow me, me, me—

From behind the dogwoods, a boy. All angles and dusk. Black haired, wild-eyed. Following him a parade of the familiar. Freckled, moon-faced, pale. Single-file and hiding from shy.

—Follow me—

—Follow me—

—Follow me, me, me—

If they notice Bo at all they don't let on — eyes fixed, high stepping across the yard. Legs rise in unison and fall forcibly to the ground. The two-four pounding ripples under the needles, loosening Bo's interlocked legs.

—Follow me—

That dark boy will become Poppa Wheelie. The king of kudzu. He'll burst through vines on his back-wheel like Evil Knievel through a ring of fire.

—Follow me—

Remie who will always smell of shit, beat to tears by his Daddy's books.

—Follow me, me, me—

The German twins who'll make Bo watch them pee.

—Follow me, me, me—

And forever-little Tobey, too pretty for his own good.

Bo holds his breath to steady himself as a hawk sweeps circles overhead. The cardinals have stopped singing. Just the hum of the box and rippling thuds. Looking over his shoulder he sees his house is still there. The water tower. The green box.

—Follow me, me, me—

Pressing the heel of his hand to his forehead helps still the throbbing. A thrown stone had opened it wide. Bo pries dried mud and blood from the cut where Brother Eli rubbed it in. "Cherokee medicine, dildo."

—Follow me, me, me—

"Get yer ass in here," yells Momma. Her disembodied head pokes from the sliding glass door. She's hiding a cigarette. "It's cold as Moses' toes." Now with a sort of sorry in her eyes.

Bo gifts a nod.

Momma sees as far as Daddy-Jim lets her. Not far these days. About here to the end of the street.

Bo can see further.

That F150 will come growling into the driveway. He'll be back and he'll be broke. Momma in the front yard, arms crossed, brow arched. A careful kiss. *You're not getting back in here unless you want to.* His hands in the air like a preacher's. *Peace be to this house.* When he says he's missed it, it'll be the God's honest truth.

Things last as long as they last.

Momma still hurts. She'll knock that bullshit truck. *Sounds like a Mexican lawn mower*, and, *one thing's for sure, Jimmy — Jesus ain't your fuckin' copilot.*

She'll circle and grin. Think she's hemmed him in. Wave her SuperSlim like she's conducting an orchestra. Then what happens, happens. Daddy-Jim's stare goes black. She'll say *you ain't a man*. It'll go deep quiet, and they'll give Bo a look that means go. And he'll go.

Bo will fall in line. Get tight with Poppa Wheelie. They'll steal tallboys from Jimmy's stash, get high on model-airplane glue, and prep the spokes of their Schwinns with Bicycle spades. Bo and Poppa Wheelie. Down mountains of asphalt they'll wobble with speed. Not a ramp high enough to keep them on the ground. Peddling frictionless over bodies far below — side by side and eyes to the sky. Over Max, and Remie, the German twins holding hands, and forever-little Tobey, who knows full well he'll eat a tire.

The march has moved to Morrow's field. Bo can still hear chanting, but not the words — a distant drumming that harmonizes with the hum of the green box and the hammering in his head.

On the other side of the duck pond — behind the tower — is a lot to explore. Brother Eli told him there are tobacco fields thick with cutworms. And horses. Dogs that will chase you. Just on the other side of the pond. The pond where the German twins will nail a catfish to a tree and skin it alive. Where Remie will proudly show his scars. Where when the seasons stop being so certain, Poppa Wheelie will misjudge the thickness of the ice.

THE STOOL READER

KYLE MERCER

It was a well-established fact in Coahoma County that Miss Evelyn Sahlsbach was never wrong about her stools.

"Midwife Extraordinaire" was how her lavender-scented business cards described the woman, her feces-reading skills credited to "Our Heavenly Father and His Boundless Blessings" in a somewhat smaller font the Beale Street printer up in Memphis had tastefully centered below Miss Evelyn's boldfaced name and contact information, as per her directive. The card's elegantly balanced design and pleasing aromatics added a professional flourish to the midwife's self-promotions but in truth were an unnecessary expense her word-of-mouth reputation for infallibly predicting a child's sex *in utero* was such that even respectable white women from as far downriver as Greenville and as far north as Tunica routinely found their way onto her weathered porch planks with a still-warm chamber pot in hand.

So when the wife of Miss Evelyn's nephew began to suspect their adolescent daughter might be dipping her monthly rags in chicken blood, the couple hastily called the midwife in to deliver her expert and discrete opinion.

"How fresh is this feces?" Miss Evelyn had asked, standing in the bedroom of the delta sharecropper's shack with the parents and the teenager, peering into a slop pot's bowl.

"Midmorning," the child's mother said. "Her regular time."

Miss Evelyn nodded her approval and set the container aside for the moment.

Popping a thermometer under the sulking girl's tongue, the midwife palpated abdomen while waiting for the instrument to register. She squeezed left and right bosoms briefly, then made a visual inspection of the nipples — large, puffy aureoled and everted affairs, as black as mocha beans — and once done with that exam, the midwife plucked her meter from its orifice, reviewed the results and turned her full attentions to the stool.

From the depths of a skirt pocket, a small amber-tinted bottle appeared. Its cap was unscrewed, a murky liquid poured out on top of the slop, the resulting mixture subsequently swirled about in much the same fashion as an oenophile might swirl a glass of vintage cabernet.

Then, with bowl lifted to nostrils, Miss Evelyn sucked in a great whiff of its odors, held the scent deep in her lungs as she conducted her analysis, eyes shut tight and head bobbing from side to side before finally delivering her verdict to both teenager and parents, informing all concerned parties that the fetus was definitely present, definitely viable and definitely female.

Worse news still: it was too far along to do anything about without putting the expectant mother's own health at risk.

The girl, upon hearing this report, offered neither protestations nor confessions, simply sat on the edge of the bed with her hands in her lap and stared out the window. Miss Evelyn found it hard to gauge her reaction, but came away with the impression the teenager wasn't too disappointed in the diagnosis. Some of the young ones were like that — they think once they have a baby, people will quit treating them like children.

Nephew and wife, on the other hand, were as mute as the girl though much easier to read. Both wore the same expressions Miss Evelyn had seen them wear the day their mule broke its leg.

The daughter was dispatched to the outhouse to dump her night soil and Miss Evelyn spoke to the parents as she packed up her things. "Nothing to be done now but make sure the girl eats right and wait," she said as she plucked the bobby pins from her uniform cap and tucked the little hat away with the rest of her gear in an ancient gunny sack she always used on discrete visits.

She cinched the bag closed and slung it over her shoulder. "I'd like to see some more green in that stool the next time I come by. And I suppose it'd be nice to know who did this to her, if you can get her to fess up."

Her nephew — a decent fellow, but not much of a talker — grunted what Miss Evelyn took to be an agreement and opened the door to the front porch for her in that gentlemanly fashion common to the era.

He was a dark-skinned man, almost mahogany in color, and his bare arms glistened where the sunlight landed on them. The wife and daughter were like that too.

Very striking.

But then all the Swindelsons — the wife's people — were dark that way. The Sahlsbachs as well, just not usually as much so.

Miss Evelyn stepped onto the porch but stopped at the farmer's stoop to admire a particularly fine example of crepe myrtle planted next to the house, then took another moment to gaze out over the surrounding acres of sharecropper land — incredibly fertile soil but constantly in need of hands to tend it.

The wife, a metal pail nestled in the crook of her arm, followed Miss Evelyn through the door on her own way to the pump.

"Shame it's not a boy," the woman said, like she was reading Miss Evelyn's mind. "A boy might've been a blessing in disguise. Frank and me ain't likely to be getting any younger." And then the missus was off to the well, without actually offering any goodbyes or thank yous.

Miss Evelyn smiled politely, because what else could one do?

The couple had had a son once, but lost him to a water moccasin. The wife had never really gotten over it and often turned unsociable when upset over even the smallest things.

Miss Evelyn felt sorry for her.

But there was nothing she could do about that old misfortune, just like there was nothing she could do about this new one.

So when the child eventually popped out months later one evening in 1952, with a noticeably unpredicted overabundance of bits and pieces poking up from between its legs, no one in the room was more dumbfounded than Miss Evelyn, who bent to examine her catch more closely, unwilling to believe her own weary eyes, the truth confirmed for her only after she had gently prodded the offending genital with a fingernail and was struck back, full-force in the face, by an erupting geyser of warm whizz.

Among the attending women in the room, there were those whose hands immediately leapt to their own faces in empathetic gestures of shock or disgust, while others attempted to stifle a snicker — with various degrees of success – responses generally divided, as opinions usually were in the family, between Sahlsbach and Swindelson sides of the clan.

But Miss Evelyn herself was neither appalled nor amused.

The midwife at that moment was preoccupied by larger concerns, the birth having already turned problematic. Decisions needed to be made and had she been looking for a divine sign to guide her just then, the urine facial was precisely the sort of omen she required: an almost baptismal-like blessing, proof positive that God himself was not only offering His approval for her to proceed with what she knew in her heart had to be done, but He was in fact aiding, abetting and conspiring with her to perform the foul deed.

Because from the instant the child had crowned and those present in the room gasped first at its much-too-pale coloring and then again, even louder, upon recognizing its features – knowing "who did this" turning out to be a thing better left unknown – Miss Evelyn had understood full well what was required of her, could clearly see the best course forward for all parties involved.

And she was not the sort of Sahlsbach that shirked responsibility.

Still, it was a nasty bit of business.

But the Lord works in mysterious ways – especially in the South – and that blessed golden shower had graced the midwife with a legitimate excuse, provided probable cause and reasonable cover, taken any need for awkward discussions off the table. So sputtering, spitting and secure in the knowledge that she was performing His will, Miss Evelyn let the boy slip out of her hands and onto its head, the infant landing at the end of its umbilical with a soft thud on the cabin's planked floor.

In hindsight, the woman's only regret would be that God had not given her enough time to first sever the cord. Had the good Lord seen fit to postpone His baptizing just a few seconds longer, she felt she might have been able to drop the boy from a far more effective height.

Why in Heaven's name the Almighty would choose to leave unfinished a job He himself had started made no sense to her. But faced with the setback, the midwife could see little recourse but to continue marching forward, like the good Christian soldier she was.

So over the sound of the dented child's screams, Miss Evelyn signaled big Cousin Itzie to herd all the attending out of the room, then proceeded to dive into the sort of awkward discussion she'd hoped to avoid, using any argument she could invent off the top of her head to prod her grandniece toward the most reasonable course of action: to convince the young mother that what had just been given birth to was not a bundle of joy but, at minimum, "a mixed-breed affront to the laws of God and nature, probably brain-damaged to boot" and — at worst — "a major white-people problem for the family that will never go away" unless the girl let Miss Evelyn do what needed to be done immediately.

"Might as well give birth to the seed of Satan's loins, as much trouble as there'll be over this one," she said, swiping runny and somewhat salty mascara as far away from her eyes as possible with one hand while scissoring at the irksome umbilical with the other, in the meantime refusing to even pick the little lad up off the floor, pretending — by means of a violent flutter of wrist — the infant's caul had burned her fingers.

But as Miss Evelyn would relate it later, in private to a trusted few, "If the girl had had good sense to start with, she would have taken care of the problem early on, and never put herself or her relations in that unfortunate situation in the first place. And lacking good sense, well . . . what could one expect?"

Their argument would conclude with the sullen teenager retreating from all proper forms of debate, limiting expressions of her opinions to indecipherable, guttural utterances and flying chunks of placenta, following which — and depending on whose side of the family one overheard describing the incident — Miss Evelyn was either escorted from the cabin by her nephew's wife and a rather large hickory stick, or else the midwife simply washed her hands of the unseemly matter and, in the words of Cousin Itzie, "two-stepped her big black booty right on out of that crazy Swindelson biddy's shack."

"There are few things on this earth that will create more trouble in one's life than trying to do the right thing," is an oft-repeated favorite among the many wise homilies Miss Evelyn has always preached.

But homily had not prepared the midwife for the ungodly amount of trouble her good intentions would wind up creating on this particular occasion.

Because in the days and weeks that followed the boy's birth, in that inevitable whirlwind of embellished eyewitness accounts, misinformed rumors and vicious — sometimes violent — Sahlsbach versus Swindelson extended-family squabbles that rumbled through the county in the incident's aftermath, requests for Miss Evelyn's ministrations and consultations suffered a plummet almost as precipitous as the child's, with even her most vocal defenders seemingly reluctant to utilize the woman's previously unassailable services.

And before three months had gone by, those troubles became so troubling the midwife would wind up seated in the rear of a Greyhound bus, bouncing and rocking toward Philadelphia.

"To assist a half-sister's granddaughter through her time," she said to the woman sitting adjacent while offering a lavender-scented card across the aisle, the stranger remarking how lucky for the expectant mother, to have such a generous and knowledgeable relative in the family and what a dear, sweet person Miss Evelyn must be.

Miss Evelyn dismissed the compliment with a modest wave of her hand, feeling it would be rude to argue the point and preferring to change the subject anyway, seeing as how there was, in fact, no half-sister, no gravid anyone, eagerly awaiting the midwife's arrival in Philly.

Still, the two ladies warmed to each other's company quickly, the stranger turning out to be a surprisingly pleasant conversationalist with an encyclopedic knowledge of gardening — next to midwifery, Miss Evelyn's greatest passion — and over the course of their cross-country journey, the women would enjoy exchanging not only the wax paper-wrapped candies and homemade tea cakes they'd brought along with them for their excursion, but also small tidbits of horticultural wisdom, acquired through decades of experience.

"I makes my own blood meal to put on my pansies in the winter," the stranger said as Miss Evelyn watched an "Entering Chattanooga City Limits" sign slide by the Greyhound's windows. "You should see the blooms I get, you ever makes your own blood meal?"

"I don't suppose I ever had much need for blood meal," Miss Evelyn countered, prying the lid from a tin container on the seat beside her. "God only knows how much afterbirth I've got buried in my yard."

Miss Evelyn passed a peppermint sweet across the aisle, then unwrapped a butterscotch for herself. "All that placenta certainly makes the fig tree happy. Some years I've been able to reach out my bedroom window and pluck sugar figs big enough to choke a horse with off those branches."

The midwife indicated the scale with forefinger and thumb, her seatmate offering an appreciative gasp.

But what Miss Evelyn did not mention in Chattanooga — or later, down the road in Knoxville or Roanoke or Baltimore — the one small tidbit she could not bring herself to share with her new acquaintance, was how just two evenings prior to purchasing her bus ticket, both Miss Evelyn's beloved fig tree, along with the house she'd been born in and called home for fifty-seven years, had burst into flame, consumed in their entirety, the latter burning all the way down to its cinder-block piers in a noticeably accelerated fashion.

She did not speak of the large hickory stick that had stood on its end in her yard, stuck in the ground like a flagpole until one of the pumper hoses knocked it over.

Miss Evelyn was not the sort of Sahlsbach that went around looking for sympathy.

But as she sat there in the back of the swaying Greyhound, tossed from side to side in the seat and sucking at a hard candy that kept sticking to her teeth — as she watched Chattanooga's gritty warehouses, greasy gas stations and "Jesus Loves You" billboards scroll past the window — Coahoma County's "Midwife Extra-ordinaire" couldn't help but suspect that if ever anyone in this world deserved a little sympathy, it would be any poor soul who'd ever tried to do the right thing.

The Desolation of Youth

/ Tyler McCurry

Excerpts from *Vanguard's* Jump Prevention Task Force

Nathan Bachman

Day 9. Rotation 133.95. Incident 103.

I'm not sure about the woman's age. I was near the starboard stern, and she was already moving through the air. I remember thinking – something has fallen from the mast. A light or scaffold. But of course, nothing falls from the mast. I know what the other watchers say now when they say it happens out of time. When they say, I'm not sure it even *happened*. It was so fast, I only see it in my memory – her legs parted, arms out, coat open and back on the wind, eyes closed. I understand what happens to the body on impact with the sea, the sheer height of the drop and the endless depths below. I have tried to imagine her swift, permanent end, but for me she's still up there, flying up and over the hull.

—William

Day 9. Rotation 133.98. Incident 104.

Was walking mid-vessel, near the university. A male adolescent climbed over the safety rails and stood poised to jump. I was fifty meters away and ran to him. He saw me, so I stopped. Stood a few meters back and began to talk. I told him my name.

"My name is Brie," I said, "and I have two boys of my own, about your age. Perhaps you know them?"

He didn't respond. Just swayed on the edge. When he closed his eyes, I was certain he was going over. I saw his fingers opening on the cables, so I rushed to him. I took hold of his left arm and then his right. He was a big boy, but he came away like an autumn leaf. I pulled him back, over the rail and onto the deck. Oddly effortless, like he had suddenly weighed less than air. He floated like helium in a balloon. Then, like magic, he regained all his mass and weight, and knocked me over. He was on his back with his eyes closed, and I had to wrestle myself out from under him. All the while, I was scolding him. I know it sounds terrible. I even hit him, slapped him across the cheek.

"You're someone's son," I told him. "Your mother's whole world. How dare you!"

He began sobbing then, so I wrapped my arms around him and rocked us, back and forth.

—Brie

Day 9. Rotation 134. Arrival Day. Incident 105.

The deck was crowded with parties and celebrations. One hundred and thirty-four rotations ago, we arrived on this planet and set sail. My grandfather crossed nine thousand lightyears to resettle an ocean. I remember, just before last rotation's Arrival Day, my whole class had gone on a field trip to see the foils from the crow's nest. We were two hundred meters above the deck and the view was the exact same. Water and more water. Nothing but horizon.

Mom wasn't happy I was out on duty for Arrival Day. I could have requested a different shift, but to be honest, I was relieved. No aunts and uncles asking how school was going, no cousins to compare futures or grades. No condescending best wishes for exams or questions about why I signed up for the task force. I can already hear my father's explanations. "Looks great on applications." He says it apologetically, loudly— so everyone around the table can hear. Then, he'll add, "It's just for a semester."

I pushed through a group of university kids and nearly fell over a picnicking couple. When the girl saw my uniform, she offered me a drink, but I declined. The entire colony must have been out on the deck. A hundred thousand people, vendors, and music, stretching the length of *Vanguard*. Two kilometers of unbroken festivities.

Up ahead, I spotted a group of kids climbing cables on the port shrouds. I ran over to them and started shouting. I recognized some from school. They were only a few rotations younger, and I think that didn't help, because they just laughed at me. I mean, before my watch, I did it myself when I was their age, climbing up the cables and looking down into the moving sea — the thrill of that moment, when you realize you've climbed so high, you can't be saved by anyone but yourself. I nearly climbed up there myself, just to share the risk. But then I think about that woman suspended, not quite overboard, not shipside. Momentarily alive. I just got so angry and began calling them names which made them giggle more until they spotted a parent or a teacher and scampered down. I know they weren't jumpers, but I decided to mention it here. After all, if one of them had gone over, what would have been the difference?

—William

Day 9. Rotation 134.03. Incident 1.

Middle-aged man. I saw him first from the starboard bow. He had all the signs. Well Dresses. Alone. Constantly looking around and heading toward the bowsprit. They always like to jump off the spar, like somehow, it's more meaningful if they throw themselves from the very tip of *Vanguard*, crushed by the waves and then obliterated underneath the massive vessel.

I doubled my pace but was careful not to run. I was just behind the man, close enough to see his balding hairline. He reached the front and almost immediately vaulted the safety railings. He was out on the spar and balancing toward the end. I clipped myself to a cable and went after him.

Most watchers wouldn't feel comfortable walking off deck, but I was a roper. I scaled the stays for a living. Twenty-five rotations of ascending the masts, hauling bolts, stress testing, repair and replace. That's how it started. In the skies of Webb-0419b, watching jumpers. From a hundred meters up, you can see the bodies impact on the sea. No screams or complaints. Just a silent eraser. We used to take bets, the guys I roped with. Who looked like they were throwing themselves off? What were the telltale signs?

I won a lot. One day, I won four bets. Four jumpers. Keller worked j-bolts and he said, "I'm done betting against Nazar. He's too good." Then he laughed, "I mean, imagine if you weren't up here."

Imagine. That was the problem. Up here. That was another problem.

At first, I just volunteered on the weekend. I figured I'd try. I stopped a jumper my first day — three by the end of the following weekend.

Five rotations later, here I am. I've seen it all — and I'm tired of seeing it.

This man wasn't any different from a dozen others, going out on the sprit to look back on the colony before hurling himself off. I call these types, romantics. Going for the grand gesture. I'm not trying to be insensitive — that's not it at all. I have other names too: bolters, exhibitionist, dither dudes, lone girls, sob bobs. I have a notebook of terms and observations because it helps. Because it works.

The gangway is narrow, and you can only place one foot down at a time, so forward momentum is important. He was careful and slow, and I figured I could overtake him before he reached the end. I was closing the distance when he went over. He didn't wait until he was at the very end, or stop to look back, just dropped off the spar. Nothing romantic about it. I'm half certain he fell on accident.

First jumper of this rotation.

We'll have to wait to ID him. I figure someone will notice his absence soon — it never takes long. Even when they live alone without family and you think, this was a nobody and so nobody will know they're gone. But someone always notices. They notice right away.

—Nazar

Day 9. Rotation 134.05. Incident 2.

It was late. The rest of the colony was asleep inside. As always, the air was balmy and bright — nothing above deck ever changes. A perpetual sunny day. Friends tell me that's part of the appeal for new colonists. I've seen them. When they arrive off transports and crowd onto the deck, smiling and opening their arms to the warmth of a close star.

I was thinking about this when Simon approached me. He introduced himself and explained he had recently fought with his wife. She stormed out, and he came here, fearful she was thinking about jumping. Following protocol, I asked for her name, to pull up photos and send it out to the other watchers on duty.

He told me it wasn't necessary. I didn't understand right away, so I insisted. Simon was visibly uncomfortable and almost walked away, so I stopped asking for his wife's name.

"Walk with me," I told him. "We'll look for her, together."

We made for the bow, scanning the deck ahead. Almost no one was out, which made things easy, but something felt wrong. Simon was quiet and gazing on the sea.

"Arnie, bless him," I said, "still drives me crazy the way he half listens — like his mind is always considering other things, and this makes me feel unimportant. His inattention is a foible, I know, but some days it feels like a catastrophic flaw. Marriage is hard that way. Eighteen rotations with the same man."

"Eighteen rotations is pretty darn good."

"Yes," I chuckled. "I suppose it is."

"Do you have kids with this Arnie?"

"Two boys in secondary. Every day is a rollercoaster."

"We talked about kids," Simon said. "We don't have any right now because Karenna isn't keen on them. She was just beginning to feel okay with her life."

I nodded along.

"For so long, she had felt trapped and useless." Simon didn't stop walking, but his eyes took on the color of the empty horizon. "Just so alone. Even with the new arrivals to the colony, this big boat out in the endless sea, isolated, pointless. Hamsters in a wheel. It took a colossal effort to push through that time, and it wasn't that long ago. With the stress and obligations of a newborn, what if those feelings returned? Or worse, what if the child grew to be haunted by these same thoughts?"

I was beginning to understand Simon, now. After all, my own children frightened me, whenever they seemed bored or anxious — like maybe Arnie and I made a mistake, choosing to bring them into the colony.

We floated on this planet in a closed loop — no escape from the uniformity of our existence. No distraction from ourselves.

"Experience is a funny thing," I said. "It's easy to assume others feel the same way, especially if they're related. I admit most days, my children feel like an extension of my body. A continuation of myself. Then, suddenly they'll do something so remote, so alien, am I reminded how impossible they are. I feel foolish even considering them my own."

We were another hour's walk to the bow. The sky was a brilliant amethyst. Simon stopped.

"I think I'll head in, take a tram back to my place," he put his hands in his pockets and began for the nearest port, then stopped. He turned, "you know, there's more phytoplankton out there then there's ever been on Earth. It isn't empty. I forget that."

I nodded like I understood because I think I finally did.

"We'll keep an eye out for your wife," I said, and he smiled. I don't know how close he was, if seeking out a watcher was a good sign or not. I've put him on the watch list.

—Brie

Day 10. Rotation 134.08 Incident 3.

Amelie Verchetti. Fourteen rotations. She had a backpack with her and a school tablet out, which is why I didn't notice her at first. She was ahead of me, walking portside toward the stern. Kids come out here to finish schoolwork all the time. They come with friends or by themselves and soak up the sun. Low risk. No indicators.

I should have thought better about the date. It was special. This ball of water is monotonous in the extreme, and yet, the scientist said the planet had just completed its tenth turn since we've arrived. Of course, we never see a change — no dusk or dawn, no night, no stars. The ocean surface freezes on the dark side which is why we never stop moving. We snail across this ball of water, matching pace with the slow churning axis, forever positioned under the white sun. One full turn; we don't even celebrate the occasion. Just a snippet in the news feeds, but symbolic dates are important. A veteran watcher should have known that.

The girl had her head down in a screen. Typical lone girl behavior. She made a turn toward the railing and then — I didn't have time. I picked up her tablet and backpack. She had written her parents and her younger brother and signed her name. Love, Amelie. I know better to pry into notes they leave behind. We're not supposed to do more than collect the things they leave, but I read it. Beginning to end.

After this week, I'm done. I know, I've said it before, but I mean it this time. It isn't natural, witnessing someone's last moments. Over and over, they drop. I'll retire from roping; I'll never step out onto the deck again. I can't sleep. In dreams, I'm crawling beneath tables, catching bottles, glasses, vases, picture frames — until my arms are so full. I try wrestling the items around so there's room for one more, fragile, breakable thing. Only, there's never enough time or space, and I can't catch the next item. I see it fall and know the sound it'll make — the terrible change as the impart ripples through the glass and erupts into a sea of glittering pieces.

In the mornings, I awake amazed that my arms are empty.

—Nazar

Day 10. Rotation 134.09 Incident 4.

Woman. She wasn't old, and she wasn't young. She saw me and made the slightest move toward the sea, so I froze. She was already off deck, sitting below the bulwark, legs hanging over the water. I was close enough to shout, so I shouted hello. It sounded stupid, but she waited. I introduced myself and began walking forward.

"What's your name?"

"Victoria," she said. "I just had a son."

"Oh?" I said.

"My friends told me when I finally see him and look into his eyes our brainwaves will sync — unconditional love, just like that. Three months. I still don't feel like his mother."

What was I supposed to say to that? I'm just some kid.

The sky was cloudless and indistinguishable from the sea. She continued, "My husband is the certain type, certain about himself and certain about the future. He doesn't even see the sea. He doesn't wonder what's beyond, you know?"

That's when I saw Nazar. He appeared behind the woman, motioning me with his hands to continue talking. I told her I wasn't certain about anything either, but I might like teaching.

"Only, my father is an important engineer," I added, and as I did, I leaned on the railing, almost causally — like I wasn't a threat to her plans. "It's expected for me to contribute to the colony in an obvious way. When I graduate, I am supposed to enroll in the science academy, but I've filled out an application for the instructor college — I always liked the idea of teaching literature. My dad thinks I'll end up in sanitation — or worse, a roper."

The woman's eyes were out on the horizon, her hand on the metal, her feet in the air. The soft push of the colony whispered below. Nazar tiptoed closer, unnoticed.

"It's the stories," I continued, not sure what I was even saying. "It's the only place you can really get off this cruise. A forest, a desert, a history of land and mountain. It's like magic, and I'd like to share that."

She looked up and smiled. "You're still young."

"That's true," I said and added a chuckle. "Now, if I can just pick the right life."

"It's this planet. It doesn't want us," she said. "Sometimes I imagine one day we'll see land. We'll finally arrive, and we'll have a real home — not some moving island we soldered together. A real, natural place meant for us."

Victoria stood then. Her hair came across her face in the moving air, and her arms were at her side. I wasn't sure if she meant to come back to the deck or to throw herself into the water. I'll never know because that's when Nazar had her. Locked his arms around her midsection and pulled her back.

Later, after we had her evaluated, her husband came to fetch her. He paused when he saw us and came over. He didn't say anything, just gave me a hug. I tried to explain it wasn't me — it was all Nazar — but when I looked to my right, Nazar had already left.

I saw him later from the windows, walking the deck.

—William

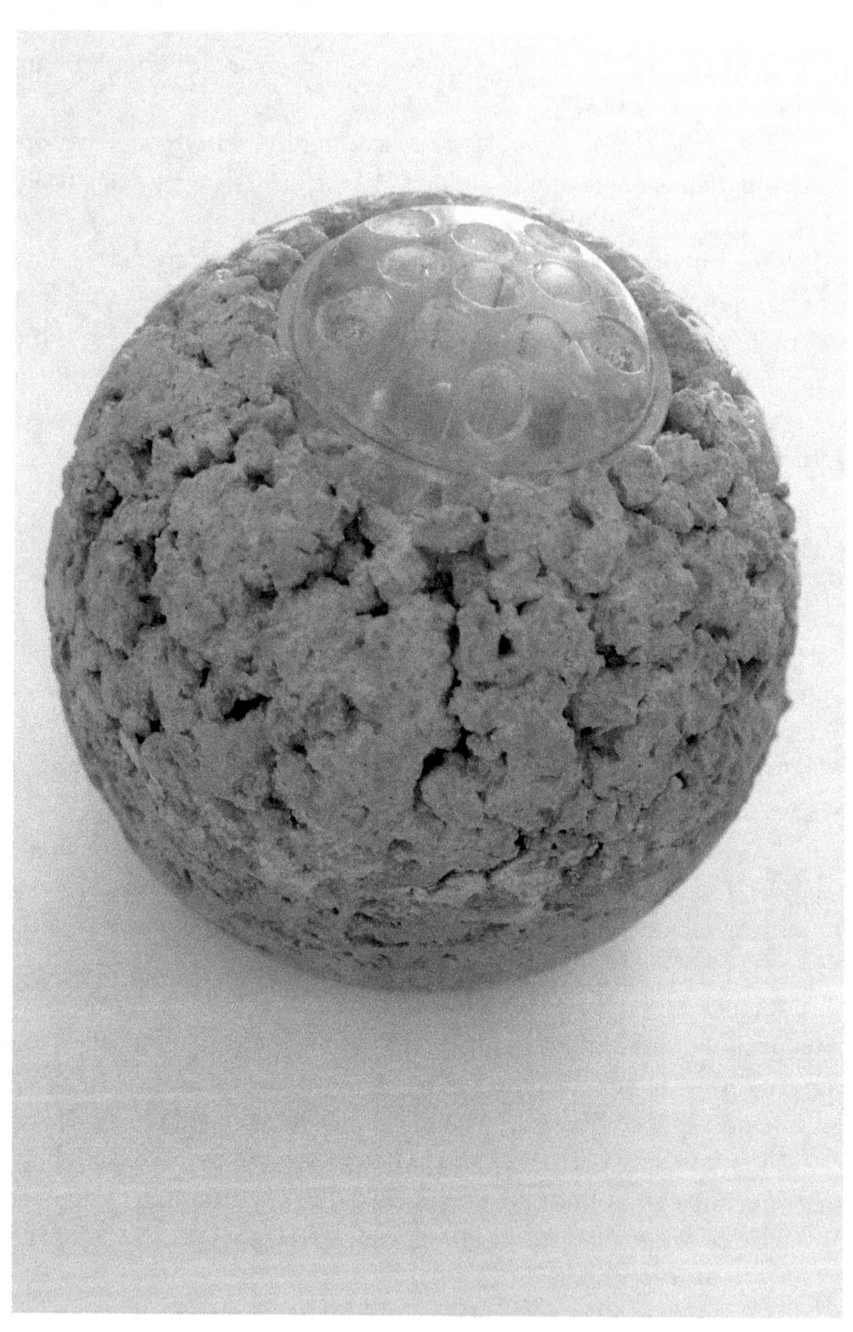

Anthroposphere 1 — Gruyere

/ Ernst Perdriel

ANTHROPOSPHERE 1 — GROYERE NEGATIVE / ERNST PERDRIEL

The Courtyard, or A Man Named Victorious

Reema Rajbanshi

The News

1.

The papers that did not report my cousin's death might have said this. Rubul Das died November 26, 2012 in Lakhimpur, a town at the edge of Assam, a state at the edge of India. He was thirty-five, a civil engineer, husband for a year and a half, father to a son of five months, son to a cancer survivor of nearly eighty, blood to two brothers and a sister, friend to the laborers who walked miles to honor him. At the Dhemaji hospital where he was pronounced dead on arrival, the doctors wrote that he'd had a heart attack. At the Lakhimpur pharmacy where his driver had rushed him, he was given painkillers and an antacid. His body was brought back to my uncle Mirza's courtyard in a plastic bag.

The relatives I met on my week-long December trip to Assam told me this. His older sister said: *I touched his face to be sure he had died. They had cut his forehead so that blood ran out. Our father, his wife stood on the side of the courtyard, looking away.* His closest brother said: *I went to the postmortem and looked into his open chest. His lungs were black, his heart and ribs covered with fat. I don't understand how this happened.* His mother said: *I told him so many times, don't eat so much meat, take your pressure pills, but I couldn't save him. In such old age, did such bad days have to come?* His father said: *They left him alone on a sofa in the pharmacy and found him with foam coming from his mouth. The one who should have died is me but the one who died was him. He must have been destined to end like this.*

I will begin telling you about my cousin like this. I called him Rubul Dada, Older Brother Rubul, but everyone else who loved him called him Ranjeet. Which means there were many people who called him He Who Wins in War.

2.

My mother had given me the news over the phone, calling from the Bronx, New York to La Jolla, California. I did not expect my own sobbing, between my low bed and papasan, my stuffing a gamoosa into my mouth.

"Reema," my mother said after a few minutes, "Reema. Listen. They already cremated him, but someone should go to Mirza."

I went beach running, but all that sand and moon and mansion sank my spirits. I gloomed out at the curling dark tide, which had washed over the eastern archipelago of rocks and anemone, and prayed for my cousin's spirit. As I shuffled back to the pavement, I crossed an older white couple sitting on the divider between sand and lot, and the woman motioned to me. "Come here."

I stood warily, barefoot on the boardwalk, and said, "What is it?"

"I just want to ask you a question," the woman said. "Are you peaceful?"

I could barely make her out in the moonlight, and the man kept his back to me, but I laughed. "I hope so."

She waved me over again. I waited.

"We were just talking," she said, "about our relatives. You see, they were complaining that they're only worth two million dollars. Well, we're only worth five hundred thousand." She stepped towards me, smiling. "What would you have said to them?"

I thought of my cousin, foaming in the back of a car, and took another step back. "I'd say money isn't everything. Money can't buy happiness or love or longevity."

"Money isn't everything," the woman beamed. "Money can't buy happiness."

"If it makes you feel better," I said, turning to go. "You're worth more than I'll ever be or people I know."

The man turned. "We're also a lot older than you are."

You are, I thought bitterly. The woman looked ready to speak but I began walking away. "At least," I waved, "you've got great company. I wouldn't worry about it."

Back in my room, I listed the passport and visa I would need for a return I had not imagined. Eight-and-a-half years earlier, I'd visited India on a year-long college fellowship to research family history. In the years after, I had left New York for California, patching together a writing life in what felt like another country. Now, I was returning to the Old, my first book undone, my mother home from a mastectomy, my sister three months pregnant, my father too close to seventy to go alone. I guessed at other questions that would greet me on that other shore: *Reema, what did you write of that year? Reema, why did it take you so long to return? Reema, how could this have happened?*

3.

All day as I waited in Indian airports — Delhi, Kolkota, Guwahati — the TV showed Delhi protests. A young woman named Damini had been gang-raped in Delhi, one of many rapes unresolved by police, but this time, Delhi exploded. Women in saris and salwars shouted in streets, holding up signs that read *Death Penalty for Rape, We Want Justice.* The Gate of India had been surrounded by furious men and women, and they in turn had been surrounded by police. Protestors were arrested; the rapists were not caught; Damini died a few days later. In each airport, closer and closer to my cousin's bone, the TVs glowed orange-red with flames in spare, fluorescent rooms.

A few months later, at a Toronto panel, where I spoke on the witch-hunting of Rabha women in Assam and Meghalaya, I listened to two other writers who had grown up in Northeast India. The non-tribal writer spoke about Irom Sharmila, a Manipuri activist who had been fasting against AFSPA in the Northeast. The tribal writer spoke about various Naga and Khasi poets who'd written about the insurgencies. Both spoke to the frequency of rape in Delhi, in India; and we all spoke about Damini, a name that meant lightning, which had been given by the public because the case had drawn so much attention.

One writer, turning in the golden light of the café, said suddenly, *It's one thing to theorize about this, it's another to live it. You have no idea.*

Which is true: I am not a tribal woman who has been raped in Delhi or another Indian city.

True too: I am Oxomiya diaspora, raised in New York City, whose luck in education and opportunity brought her to this page.

Also true: I am Rajbongsi, which means my father's people are native to Lower Assam, and live there still. As an Asian-American woman, I have an idea or two about size and silencing.

In the end, true: I can only speak for who I was, traveling for a year through Northeast India on fellowship, and who I'd become, nine years later, saying goodbye to the cousin who'd wanted to ensure I would have no idea about violences I'd learn anyway.

4.

The family had stored my cousin's hip bone in a bamboo reed stuck into a pot. The bone was where he had fallen. The pot was kept in the back of a thatched shed between the house and the garden. In this shed, in front of my cousin's bone, there is a dheki, that quintessential Oxomiya beam, perched on a peg, which works like a pendulum to grind food. You must pump a dheki with your leg while the other end mashes whatever you place in a smooth earthen hole. Rice, sesame, dal. It was only after I watched my cousin's oldest brother pump the end with his leg, while my aunt (facing my dead cousin's bone but not facing it) swept spilled ground flour back into the hole, that my female cousin pointed out the pot.

"That is your Rubul Dada," she said.

I started and she pointed to the clay lamp beside the pot. "Every morning, his wife lights it. You can photograph this if you want."

But after photographing my cousin nine years before, warm and bubbling, how could I record him, like this, now?

Trysts

1.

The photo I remember most of our Upper Assam trip, Rubul Dada hadn't known I'd snapped. A shy photographer, I'd shot from the back Rubul Dada and his friend, Chintu, walking down a wooded Sibsagar road. Rubul Dada wore a white jacket, Chintu a purple one, and the road ahead was a black ribbon, the arc of trees high and green. We had just come from looking at our first Ahom structure, a reddish dome that, the sign read, the Ahom had made from a mortar of clay and eggshells. *Look how it has lasted hundreds of years!* we said.

Not just that dome but Talatal Ghar, the Sibsagar fort with its Mughal-style arches, its buried levels, its sprawling bends that maybe hid soldiers, spies, princes. The fort was a miracle — made from a humble mortar of eggshells and rice grain that had withstood the stalwart empire before the Brits' — and zigzagged in a maze that hinted at cunning war choreography. We walked along the few levels above ground, and it was like passing through haunted corridors, other levels hidden below us, other bodies hidden by time. We ran our hands along the black cannons, the bumpy red walls, the creviced brick where perhaps poetry as well as politics had been blasted.

I ran into Chintu on my goodbye trip, nine years after that Sibsagar outing. I was walking down a local Mirza road buzzing with folks and dogs and scooters, when he turned from a roadside stand. There was only the dim light of the stand that threw its circle on us. We stared. We said nothing. My sister-in-law introduced him to me, then we nodded, said we knew each other. He had married too, looked about the same with a few extra pounds, but now we stood in an unexpected corridor, a new ghost between us.

2.

The first broadcast that went across a free India had been Nehru's, right after the British withdrew, August 14, 1947:

> "Long years ago we made a tryst with destiny, and now the time comes when we shall redeem our pledge, not wholly or in full measure, but very substantially . . . A moment comes which comes but rarely in history, when we step out from the old to the new, when an age ends, and when the soul of a nation, long suppressed, finds utterance . . . We think also of our brothers and sisters who have been cut off from us by political boundaries, and who unhappily cannot share at present in the freedom that has come. They are of us and will remain of us whatever may happen, and we shall be sharers in their good and ill fortune alike."

I had seen Nehru, in an elegant kurta with that buttonhole rose, uttering this promise as a kid in the Bronx, on some Indian TV channel. Even then, his triumphant English, the crackling bass under the repeated *tryst-pledge-freedom* made me shiver. Where was my maternal grandfather that midnight, my Ata who had been jailed by the British for being a freedom fighter, a Communist? Had my parents, my Peha and Pehi, who must have been country babes then, tingled with a whirring sense of change?

All those trysts with my cousins in their Mirza courtyard, I had not thought of Nehru's words but our own, heated in what seemed simple games. Mostly, my cousins had twisted and swung slender limbs to the rhythms of cricket, a game I learned most Indians adored, a game it seemed my cousins could master. I had to beg the boys to let me play, and when they ignored me, pitching low balls that made wobbily runs past the shed, into the back garden, I sulked on the courtyard steps. The one time they relented to my scowls, Rubul Dada pitched the ball into my jaw. Of course, I ran off wailing-all-hell, and my cousins scattered across the burning courtyard. To hide the culprit ball, to tiptoe sheepishly round the kitchen, to wait till my aunt stopped scolding from the meal table. There I sobbed, betrayed, as she patted me down with black tea, a warm towel to my swollen cheek. It was Mintu Dada who brooded over first, sitting beside me and crying at my tears. And it was Tapan Dada and Rubul Dada who went out and brought bangles back to where I curled, behind a mosquito net on their bed.

So sorry, Rubul Dada said in English, offering in his palm the heavy cricket ball. *Take this. You hit back. But please, if you stay mad, I will feel bad.*

3.

The biggest spat Rubul Dada and I had — and we had several — erupted when we went to visit tea gardens in Upper Assam. All along the jeep ride through the gardens, green expanses on both sides, he and his friend giggled about the surprise they had in store for me. Each time I demanded they tell me what the surprise was, they knowingly glanced at each other, said, *No, she'll get scared*, then laughed again.

The surprise was that the professor had arranged a Christmas Eve visit to a Naga village. The village chief's son, who would show us around, was once a member of the insurgent outfit, the National Socialist Council of Nagalim. I wasn't scared, I thought resentfully as I huffed behind the two boys up a hill; I was unprepared — no gifts, no questions, no nothing. The village was at the top of a foothill and, on our two-hour trek there, we paused several times to gulp in air. The soil was muddy, with steps sometimes cut into it, sometimes not, so that when we slipped, our jeans were brushed with swaths of ochre. Halfway up, we came upon a gazebo, which gave us a view of the plains we had left, and the contrast between that flat tan maze and these palm-and-sun dappled hills was startling.

On our excursion back up, the chief's son met us — a slender, solemn-faced guy, in his thirties — who said we were late, he had worried, he had in fact made the up-down trip twice to find us. With our tomato faces, our sweaty limbs, we laughed. Did a revolutionary look so utterly ordinary, so surprisingly delicate?

What filters as important now about that trip is how my cousin too wandered about in wonder. Through the long log school newly built for the village children, strung up with Christmas lights and shiny paper words, where the children would also learn English. Across the field where we finally sat under a tree and watched children playing traditional games: spearing grapefruit, shooting bows, and watching us strangers back. Then settling in the drawing room of our Assamese driver, who had been our go-between, enjoying me strike up a chat with the Naga girl who spoke English.

Maybe he remembered how much ragging I'd gone through at my Guwahati hostel, mostly with the Upper Assamese tea garden girls. How only the Naga girls had befriended me, bringing hot jilabi to my room, taking me out to eat momos, watching movies together in all our rooms, whether in

English or Hindi. *Look at her go*, my cousin smiled. *She's never that excited with us.* I'd rolled my eyes at him. But what I remember now is how the girl, named Seven in Sema, told me about her brother who had died in his twenties. He had contracted malaria and been taken to Guwahati Medical, she said, where he had been given the wrong medicine. She said it so plainly, as we stood before the mound where his body had been buried.

My cousin's sister later said, to my stunned face those first few days back, *It's like a fast-forward cut in a film reel, isn't it?* Yes, except this was suddenly life and the schoolhouse lesson learned late was some of us do not walk away alive.

What I remember now too, and regret, is the essay I wrote and published, in *Luitor Pora Mississippi* in 2006, detailing that trip. I do not regret recounting the generosity of our Sema Naga hosts, the tragicomic food bumble between the professor, the other Assamese guests, the Naga chief's son, but how I had berated my cousin for letting his friend pull such a stunt without asking me.

It's my time, I had cried as my cousin slumped on a bed in the tea estate. *And my money!*

Yes, yes, he said quietly. *I'll talk to him. You're right.*

No, I would say now. *Why didn't you call me out?* Why didn't you say it's *our* stories, *our* time you're borrowing? Because look, how for no good reason, I again ended up with more of both. How that Christmas Eve, strangers took us in, tea garden girls draped a gamoosa round my neck before they danced jhumur for me, how the singer came and sang, full-throated, though he had been sick in bed for days. How I have no idea as I write this where any of you are.

4.

Here are two women Rubul Dada found beautiful: Aishwarya Rai, Kareena Kapoor. He and Chintu sat in their friends' empty bedroom, on mornings we lounged about before exploring Upper Assam, and watched Bollywood films that constantly ran on TV. I slurped my spicy fried noodles on the bed while they gushed on the floor about Aishwarya, as long as a crane (and about as limber), dancing to the lemon song.

She's so lucky, my cousin said. *Born beautiful and talented and rich.*

Kareena Kapoor, he had actually seen, in his time traveling through Mumbai. We were walking through Upper Assam ruins on yet another hill when I asked what she looked like.

Very beautiful, he said, shaking his head as if it were a disturbing truth. *More beautiful than even in cinema. But it was hard to see her with the cameras around her.*

I watched him walking about the circular stone remains of Aniruddha's house. Short and dark like me, he'd always liked the light, North-Indian looking girls. No surprise, then, when nine years later, I met his widow: a pale, willowy creature who seemed to transfer her iron grief to her dark, twisty-lipped baby.

Rubul used to say, she told me, *we'll have to pay this one ek lakh to see his smile.*

He had told me, nine years before, about a girl he had known for years, a love at first sight thing that it had taken several years of courage-and-courtship to make real, but I hadn't met her then. Goalpara was not pressing on my itinerary, and there had been violence between Assamese purists and Assamese who had absorbed some Bengali culture. Now here she was, by day solemnly bathing and nursing their son; by night, weeping over her inexplicable fate, a love of sixteen years gone, a baby of five months left, a young widow about to start a government job.

How could my cousin and I have foreseen all this, walking about one of the most fabled architectures of Assam's City of Romance? It was in Tezpur, legend has it, that the princess Ukha fell in love, in a dream, with Aniruddha, Krishna's grandson. Her artist friend, Chitralekha, cast her magic to call Aniruddha to Ukha, but Ukha's father, the Bana Raja, built a fort to keep the lovers apart.

It was in that fort, nine years ago, Rubul Dada told me about the woman he hoped would become his wife. Nine years later, it was in my uncle's courtyard, circled by a brick wall, where I walked with my cousin's widow and son.

Who is the Bana Raja in this story? Is Chitralekha real?

Rajdhani Express

1.

Every marginal Indian's favorite "terrorist" movie, *Dil Se*, is also the only Bollywood movie I've seen with a train running through Assam. The movie's first song has the good Delhi boy Raj, played by Shah Rukh Khan, dancing *chaiya chaiya* on a train moving through mellow hills, next to some sexy-naveled girl, against a backdrop of Assamese natives and their japis. It is a morning train that brings Raj, still hopeful, still naïve, to what will turn out a deceptive paradise. For the romance between the North Indian patriot and the Assamese insurgent Moina, played by Manisha Koirala, can only end with a hug that blasts them to bits. Raj, it seems, dies because his heart is too big, but what of the impossible loves at the nation's edges, like the one my cousin's widow bears? What if Raj dies not because Moina's heart is so disfigured but because it has been broken so badly?

It is a scene nothing like a train blocked by protestors lying on the rails. I had first seen that image on Indian news sites, summer 2012, while home. After violence broke out between Bodo people and Bangladeshi Muslims in Kokrajhar district, and after the Center had once again responded too late, thousands of folks had blocked the passage of the Rajdhani, a train that connected Delhi, the Indian capital, with Guwahati, the state capital. The papers framed the event as typically disastrous of the Northeast, yet I found the image remarkable, a testament to the people of the region stopping, for a few hours, the brutal brush of "Royal Rule" past them.

The incident, which ended in the largest displacement of South Asians since 1947 Partition, made it to the New York Times front page about a month later. By then, anti-Northeast violence had spread across India, with some Muslims arguing they had to retaliate for the regional attacks on Muslims; and so millions of panicked Northeast Indians boarded trains from major cities back to the edge, back to home. I remember copying the front-page story for my parents in our local Bronx library, the Dominican librarian bragging to the lady librarians how he had once dated a half-Muslim girl, the mostly black and Latino students clicking diligently on computers, the mostly Jewish old-timers gossiping over chess boards. I folded the warm paper into my knit bag and wondered: how many of us had landed to this city edge by such violences?

At our kitchen table, my parents mused over the story, noting that for once the description was nuanced, mentioning land as much as religion. Then they parted for the rituals that comforted them each: my mother washing the dishes, my father googling the week's weather.

Now they're blaming, I joked to my mother, *Rajbongsi manu for the violence.*

We laughed as my father, half-smiling, focused on the digital clouds.

Ey, did you hear, my mother asked my father.

They'll blame whomever, my father said scornfully, and we laughed again.

What else was there to do?

2.

I found out about the other deaths, deaths I had not even heard of in California, when Pehi handed me the photo album. There was a photo of Rubul Dada, leaning slyly against Peha's mother, who inexplicably wore shades with her white widow's sari. He had draped his right arm about her tiny shoulders and crossed his legs, debonair and grinning. Then there was a photo of my cousin standing behind a sofa of people: two girl cousins married in Tihu. Again, he had draped his arms about one center woman, resting his chin on top of her braided hair. He was not smiling impishly but even in those large, gentle eyes, there was light.

What happened to Bhindeu? I asked my cousin's closest brother, and I pointed to the dark-skinned man beside the center woman, her husband. I remember him at two different points: once, in grade school, when he had served my family tea with the jittery hands, rheumy eyes of a drinker; again, in 2003 at a wedding, when he came with my cousin and his two children, looking gaunt but sober.

Didn't you hear? Tapan Dada said, pacing the verandah. *He was hit by a train and died instantly.*

What? When?

Last year. The Rajdhani. It goes so fast you don't hear it until after it's passed you. He was climbing back onto his train after getting something to eat, and it killed him.

Instantly?

Tapan Dada stared at me and circled a hand about his head. *Shaved off the whole back part.*

Where was he going?

The Rajdhani always comes from Delhi. It goes to various cities. This one was going back to Guwahati. If only he hadn't gotten off to eat.

3.

Back before I understood this history, Rubul Dada had seemed like any traveler on their way. More clearly now, he had been the trickster Dada at whom I raged even as I craved his attention. The Dada who had eyes so large and lashed, they looked like a girl's. The Dada who loved eggplant, as I did, eating it any way my Pehi made it: sliced and fried with turmeric, or mashed with mustard oil, onion, and cilantro, or grilled and spiced alongside river fish fritters, mopping it all with his expressive hands. The Dada who always wore his button-down shirts outside his pants, so that they seemed nighties on his small frame, with the long sleeves rolled up, just as my father wore them. The Dada who clowned so incessantly, teasing me about my accent, my looks, my temper till I blew up, yet who ran to the well to hide his tears as I was about to leave for the airport. The Dada who made his parents and mine brag about his engineering job, the first on his father's side to mix and stay in the middle class after centuries of farming land that had once been Kochari but had then been owned by upper-caste zamindaars. The Dada who had spoken more languages than us all, seen more of India than we had, a cosmopolitanism Northeasterners were assumed too shy, too poor to possess. Yet he had, like my father and uncles, tried to go back, something Oxomiya people, even if they won't say so, couldn't overlook. Rubul Dada was loyal and loyalty, as Northeasterners know, is a material and mystifying mark of love.

4.

I'd rather not end by imagining what it was inside that may have killed my cousin. I'd rather end by imagining my cousin enjoying a train like Shah Rukh Khan had, when he toured the nation that sometimes claimed us, sometimes didn't. I'd rather see him finally as in those photos of him and his friends in Goa, in Mumbai, in Jaipur, relaxed and aligned before those marvelous forests and sands and palaces that, at least in those moments, he could claim back. I'd rather imagine him being — as he too flirted with strange girls, drank his fill of chai in the rain, felt the freedom of coming and going — just another ordinary body along for an ordinary trip.

Boat Brothers

1.

Let me tell you a story about brothers and sisters.

My mother's oldest brother was a tall, handsome guy who flitted about town, chatting up the ladies, milling with men around fires. He took his youngest sister, my mother, out to lunch to curb the disdain of the other girls, who would not speak to this astonishingly white, well-off girl, and to ward off the eyes of other guys, who always asked why his sister wasn't yet married. Mama himself flirted with every tempting woman, a regular Krishna, but for whom did he save the choicest concert tickets, the latest saris, the freshest sweets?

Like this, Ma and Mama attended a concert Bhupen Hazarika gave after his own brother, Jayanta Hazarika, died at thirty-four. My mother remembers sitting beside her brother, in the red sari he had given her, as Bhupen Hazarika sang the verses he had once sung with Jayanta. He wept as he pumped that harmonica, singing to a brother also gifted, also a drinker, but who had not made it.

How did it happen, I asked my mother. *Assamese people say it was drinking but the Internet doesn't list a cause.*

People say it was food poisoning, my mother said. *But he died in Kolkata, not Guwahati. When someone dies far away, people can say anything.*

A couple months after that concert, my uncle died. The truck he had been driving crashed and he came home not knowing his gut ache was a burst kidney. By the time he pissed blood, by the time my mother and grandmother rode with him to the hospital, he was too full of poison. He died in my mother's lap. He had had the rare love marriage, and his two girls were still infants.

When Rubul Dada died, it was the daughters-in-law who picked up the first calls for identification; but the commissioner called Tapan Dada and that's how everyone knew it was grave. It was Tapan Dada, who had been like Rubul Dada's shadow, who learned that his other self had died. The light-skinned, green-eyed brother learned that the dark-skinned, brown-eyed brother had died. The serious, practical brother learned that the emotive, prankster brother had died. The home-bound, teacher brother learned that the roaming, engineer brother had died.

It was Tapan Dada who had called me in La Jolla, so I might speak to the driver who had come to Mirza for the last rites, an apologetic man who kept saying, *sister, I did my best*. It was Tapan Dada, curt and quiet on the phone, who read the names of the medicine the doctor had given Rubul Dada, mostly unrecognizable, mostly antacids. It was Tapan Dada who described his brother's open chest, black and fatty, as I ironed my salwar in his room.

Have you gotten the final report? I asked.

Nai powa.

Why not?

He kept watching me iron. *That's the way things are done here.*

Call me when you get it. Are you sure it was just a heart attack?

We talked about opening a case. But our father said, what's the point? That won't bring him back.

2.

In the 60s, to allay the bloodshed between the Assamese and Bengalis, Bhupen Hazarika penned an Assamese variation on his friend Paul Robeson's song, *We Are In The Same Boat, Brother*. Bhupen Da, or Older Brother Bhupen as people called him, wrote hundreds of songs about Northeast India, an upside-down heart of seven states most Indians cannot name. As a girl in

NYC, I remember only the Rubin Museum of Himalayan Art showing the Northeast within whatever gilded frame showed India. But Bhupen Da not only sang about the Assamese, he sang about who we were in our bones: a rural people, a folk culture, a mixed nation of tribal and non-tribal, a people losing land and life to many kinds of wars.

I had heard my father singing this song with two uncles, in half jest-and-joy, when some wedding or convention threw our small numbers together. Like many of their generation, these three were professionals who had come to America after the 1965 quota on Asians had been lifted. Men like them, lucky as well as scrappy, often return to the places that haunt them. My father: a civil engineer to a village where kids chased down drivers, crying *car!* Das Uncle: a surgeon whose toilet humor was the only thing that had my father rolling off the couch, to an even sparer village in Pathsala. Lohit Uncle: an electrical engineer and adrenalin junkie, who'd been found, as a baby, by the edge of the Brahmaputra River.

So my father flew us to Assam every few years, mostly to Pehi, his youngest sister. What I remember first is the monsoon in Pehi's courtyard. It fell like a barrage of bullets — the house shook — my sister and I ran out to the courtyard slashed a hundred times with sideways rain. We clutched the columns, shivered in our dresses, and wondered: how were we supposed to play? How were we supposed to see India? How were we supposed to see anything at all? My cousins, used to all this, laughed.

We played game after game of karam or spinning top or U.S. versus India, in my cousin's bedroom. The Mississippi versus the Brahmaputra, the President versus the Prime Minister, two hundred fifty years of history versus thousands. Rubul Dada, in those days, built house after house of paper and cardboard, which he'd spend weeks painting. They were variations of houses he'd seen in the city, far bigger than my uncle's, though no dogs because, Dada complained, they ate better than poor people did. My father and uncle shook their heads at my cousin's houses, which lay about in corners of the real house, unfinished. *Engineering*, everyone told him, *was like architecture but more stable.*

What grew clear over the years was how we'd grown alongside and away from each other. Tapan Dada would swing onto his truck, heading to Meghalaya for lumber, or onto his scooter, zipping to Bijoynagar to teach. Mintu Dada, my melancholy brother, my favorite brother, would be holed up in his room, mooning over some lost job or girl or song. My sister receded completely from these scenes, ensconced in her Manhattan commute-and-company, while I wrote stories in California, between teaching, waitressing, nannying, and library-servicing. But Rubul Dada, my Pehi's favorite, was still tweaking her ears, still tampering with dishes in the kitchen, still skipping easily between courtyard and street and back. So many friends to see, so many boys calling from the road, on the phone: *Ranjeet ase na? Is Ranjeet there?*

Because no matter where else bombs were bursting, my uncle's courtyard was a country of air and light. About a 10 x 20 rectangle of concrete, it had a shifting cover of sun-rain-star, a brick wall that kept it neat from the street. The other three courtyard sides were made of the wall to my cousin's game room, the wall to the family drawing room, and an entire side of steps to the other connected rooms. Smooth grey steps where my aunt would sit shucking rice or descaling fish, while Rubul Dada hung off a column, joking or singing or muttering. His good-time energy buoyed up the place when he was there, and when he was not, the house was waiting, its courtyard awash with sun but not his sweetness.

That *goodbye* visit, my female cousin and I lingered by the courtyard gate, as she explained how Bhupen Da's boat song came to be. Bhupen Hazarika, she said, was asked to pen something right there at the concert, and the Robeson he riffed on became the song asking for reconciliation. This my cousin said with eyes burning up at a house with broken windows. Stones had been thrown during those Assamese-Bengali language riots, and my aunt and uncle had not repaired them. They had chosen the spaces left by shards to tell a story. My cousin, playing this song, was choosing hope over hate.

We're in the same boat, brother.
If you shake one end, you gonna rock the other.
It's the same boat, brother.

Except I no longer believe we are in the same boat, or that some folks have a ticket onto anything in the first place, or that a song as melodious as Bhupen Da's could have saved a man named victorious. I'm a wary woman, rarely forgiving, and nine years has taught me that plenty of us, given a thrilling enough horror show, will pause our oars to watch our own kin drown. Yet in that winter of protests alighting old cities, of ashes blowing through open squares, I felt moved, alive on a boat propelled by so much remembrance, such surprising faith.

3.

Sunny afternoons, my cousin's widow, Ona Bou, bathed their son, Baba, in the courtyard. She put out a tie-dye-colored plastic bin and washed him in the clear sun. A somber baby who hardly made a peep, he livened up at this excursion, splashing his paws in the water, blinking the large dark eyes that were my cousin's. Ona Bou seemed easier in these moments too, smiling once in a while, waving at me to come closer, snap a pic.

I had taken many pics, nine years earlier, of Runuma Ba's son, the first baby born to my four Mirza cousins. I was the one with the Pentax, the nebulous aim of writing about Northeast India, and here he was, this lotus-eyed babe as round as a frog, as prized as life. So I'd shot him, Baba then too, as the Assamese call their baby boys, as my cousin had always been called by his family: taking his first bath, in his naming ceremony, watching his first bihu, that dance of our new year. Bhindeu, my brother-in-law, stood patiently in so many of these pics, eyes shining as he held up his son. But in these new photos, my cousin was the ghost, the one who should have been there, instead of his widow with her pink eyes, his brothers with their grave faces, my uncle with his sudden gaunt frame.

The other three boys felt it too, though only the oldest, the Baba of nine years before, understood. Mintu Dada's nine-year old son was the chatty one who had taken a liking to me, bringing me back half his school lunch, visiting me in my room to try my fingerless gloves, my lotion, my comb. He was the one who leaned over the baby's crib and declared — *your father's not coming back, did you know that?* — till my cousin scolded him away. The other boy, only two, looked like a Kochari with his tipped eyes and moon face, and unfortunately, acted like the tribal stereotype. Whatever you want to call it, naughtiness or daring, he ran everywhere, tumbling down those steps, wailing over egg-sized lumps before he tried climbing out a window or swashbuckling a knife longer than he was.

But my sisters-in-law loved those babies so hard, never spanking them, hugging them as if that would help them breathe, letting them run free, free, free. The rare time they put the Kochari in the bamboo crib in the courtyard, he screamed as if his life depended on it, and I joked that he was crying *Azadi! Mujhe azadi jahiye! Freedom! I want freedom!* Which made me wonder, glancing at the bedroom where either Ona Bou or Baba would cry, can you love someone hard enough for two? Would Baba learn to stay quiet or to scream? Would he always be different, and did he already sense why?

The only origin story that became clear was this: my cousin's home name, Rubul, had been given by my Communist uncle after the Russian currency. That when Rubul Dada had been born, my uncle had been hopeful, in an India about as old and independent as my cousin would be when he died in it.

4.

On a 2003 bus ride out from Majuli, once the world's largest river island, I sat beside an Assamese man who asked me about my trip. I told the stranger about visiting a Mising village, about going into a sang-ghar (a traditional tribal house built on sticks above the river), about bargaining for hand-woven shawls, about photographing two Mising women, one young and beautiful, the older one's defined cheekbones and nut-brown skin reminding me of my grandmother's face.

What do you think, the stranger asked, *aren't they pigs?* I started at his bluntness, even though I expected this in India, but still . . . really?

Their homes are cleaner than Guwahati's, I said.

He squinted at me, the way I'd sometimes seen Upper Assamese or general assholes do when I flipped the script. *Traitor!* (Which I'd heard.) *Kochari!* (Which I'd also heard.)

What is important now about that conversation is how, the next time I'd see a sang ghar, it would be to honor a more dire crossing. My sister-in-laws wanted to commission for me a metalwork picture of a sang ghar, but carrying that memory felt impossible. Rubul Dada and I had sat together in the Majuli sang ghar's shaded bedroom, over a delicate floor through which we could see the hungry river. He had sat haggling with the Mising boy who'd brought us there, while I'd nagged Rubul Dada to leave it alone, to let them take whatever price they could get.

Even this one flash of firmness from my cousin seemed funny, he who had mocked things more than usual on that first river crossing. He had mocked our auto-rickshaw driver who, when the rickety auto chortled to a stop, knelt on the ground and prayed to the auto god. He had mocked the sinuous bamboo bridge that was the only visible way to cross a sudden tributary flanked by heavy trees. We stood, me-my cousin-his loud friend, gazing out at this exquisite antiquity.

Let's go, I said, setting a foot on that bridge.

Bye, my cousin said cheerily. *And when you fall into the middle of that water, I'll be standing here waving. Bye!*

He mocked the satra members who woke, every chilly morning, at six to bathe in icy water. *No heating*, he announced to me that first morning. *Wake up and experience the authentic Assam!*

When I made a face and mumbled I'd rather wait, he pinched his nose and said, *oh-, ho-ho, you want everyone to be saying, who is that pretty, stinky girl?*

But he didn't mock me when, on the way back, we ran into a Spanish couple who could speak neither English nor a single Indian language, but whose navigational phrase was *I love India!* Good enough for my cousin, who grinned *yeaahhh*, gave a thumbs up, and said, *we love India too!* So I spoke slowly in Portuguese to this couple who spoke slowly in Spanish. We spoke about Vaishnav Hinduisim's founder, Sankar Dev; we spoke about how Indians picked up quickly on foreigners, but differently; for the blonde, blue-eyed Spaniard, he'd been touched and questioned, the object of fascination; for his brunette girlfriend, she'd been shepherding them like a determined pilgrim through this other holy land; for me, who got derided on the street by boys who called me an Assamese pretending to be American, till I opened my mouth; we spoke about new year's rituals, how the Spanish put twelve grapes in their mouths for each midnight stroke, how the Assamese celebrated by another calendar entirely, in the spring and for a whole month, but burned tall huts and ate pithas for January's Magh Bihu. The whole time, my cousin, who spoke Assamese, English, Hindi, and other Indian languages, but not these European ones, watched me with his eyes shining.

But it is my cousin's crossing, not to that eroding island but away from it, that has made me feel, most unexpectedly, the Portuguese word *saudade*. How you can miss something with deep blueness, how you can learn only in missing how much you loved, so that months later you will be driving in sunny San Diego and suddenly, for the long pause of a red light, you weep, the water your cousin threatened washing your face.

Destiny

1.

Back in my San Diego apartment, cross-legged in a square of sun, I sat typing in a sudden FB chat with a Guwahati friend. He had visited my Mirza week, sitting in the drawing room and sipping tea while my uncle and his own father talked about the political and economic rubble of Assam. Eight years earlier, I had sat with Rubul Dada in drawing rooms much like that one, in Assam, in Arunachal, and had listened about other boys lost to war or poverty or drugs. I had not imagined I would be hearing my cousin's name among theirs.

Over FB, across oceans, my Guwahati friend launched into what he had held back in that drawing room. *You have to write*, he said, *about the real India.*

I'm trying, I said.

Now with the Delhi protests, he said, *the world will see how sick this place is.*

You mean the rapes?

Everything. The only way to survive here is to be corrupt. Good people either end up begging on the road or dead.

2.

The third night of my *goodbye* visit, my eldest cousin, Mintu Dada, scootered me and his four-year-old son to a nearby kabadi game. A wrestling game of touch-me-not, marked by a simple chalk line, I had first played this in my uncle's courtyard. It had seemed alarmingly raw — no props, not much strategy, just the brute agility of your body — and I always lost. That night, at least a hundred boys scuffled across rectangles chalked off in a green school field. Though these teenagers strutted up and down, wrangled and thumped limbs and heads, they seemed so unjustly outweighed that I found the spectacle, through all the kicked-up dust, disturbing.

Mintu Dada led us to the front row, where I gripped my nephew on my lap, first before a game of Tongla versus Silchar, then before a game of Mongoldoi versus Nalbari. The boys tussled hard, cheered on by their mates, and sometimes crashed out of the rectangle right into our row. Not only was the game removed from the American imagery of hulking footballers, tall tennis players, it was like an easy array of the Northeast's bewildering diversity. There were the tribal boys of Tongla, perhaps Bodo, against the Bengali boys of Silchar. There were the Upper Oxomiya boys of Mongoldoi, perhaps some Ahom among them, against the Lower Oxomiya of Nalbari, not far from my parents' hometowns. Of course, there must have been somebody on each team to throw out easy essentializing, to point to how much we moved to-and-fro across lines, like the wild skidding of kabadi.

On the way back to his scooter, my cousin talked about being Koch. *You know that's what we are, right?* he said. *Of course,* I said. It had been one of the unforgettable discoveries of my fellowship year. He expanded on how we were part of that indigenous group but that some of us, like my father's family, had been mainstreamed into Assamese society. *There are still Rajbongsis,* he said, *who speak their own language. But not us*, he laughed, tossing his son onto the scooter. *We've become Assamese.* I could understand why, thinking of so many groups in so many places who had made this choice. *But,* he said as he waited for me to get on behind his son, *the mark is still there.*

3.

Maybe it boils down to accidents all along. If I had been born not to my father but to my aunt, the sibling who was pulled out early from school because she was a girl, she was needed at home, she was to be married, and if my cousin had been in my stead, would he be alive? Would I?

My father, on my return, said fondly as he washed the dishes, how my aunt had had the sharpest memory of them all. How she hadn't wanted to leave school at all. I told him, as I tore the crumpled kolasapori pitha he had made, how she had wanted to learn to read English while I was there.

How she had remembered my long feet and long nose as a baby. How she had recited the story of me being *botmas*, at three imitating a neighbor who'd daily call the lame villager to eat. My cousin had had my aunt's twinkly humor, though his was laced with a boy's jabs. How many times had we fought, him fuming and muttering off to his room, me throwing myself sullenly onto a hard bed? He resented me, I knew: the luxury of my rage, what must have seemed my unearned coldness, when he'd had to deploy far more charm to approach half the things I was given. He adored my sister, I knew: she who laughed at his tricks, she who was fair and floaty the way he liked, she who was always game to ride behind him as he scootered off from friend to friend on dirt roads.

The last week of that goodbye trip, my uncle took me into the drawing room alone and told me this last story of my cousin's love for my sister: how he had been so excited to meet her and her husband, a Goan-American who'd never been to Assam, that he'd talked about taking them to Kaziranga. Kaziranga, Assam's famous wildlife park for riding an elephant to spot the tigers, the rhinos, is a place we'd all gone to together; though we hadn't gotten the elephant ride that winter because, as was typical in India, some "VIPs had come that day and wanted them." My sister had hung a photo of her and Rubul Dada, hands on hips, mugging before the bulbous red sunset.

He was supposed to go there, my uncle said, *the week he died. He had made plans to be there, but when your sister cancelled coming, he went to work instead.*

I mentioned this to my sister, who said, *yes, it's been a long time, but I have sweet memories of him.*

I didn't tell her what my uncle said, for which I had no reply. *So I think, if your sister cancelled, if your parents couldn't come, then this was his destiny.*

4.

The evening before my flight back, I sat again on the courtyard steps, watching new boys playing cricket. Mintu Dada and Tapan Dada threw the ball to my oldest nephews, nine and four, who kept missing and shrieking. Runuma Ba sat beside me, watching as I slumped in that courtyard, all of us steeped purple and grey in the quick-falling dusk. She thumbed through her phone and paused on a Bhupen Hazarika song I had heard growing up, a song I had not noticed was sung with his brother, Jayanta. The gentle lyrics, the husky voices took on, like that yard and sky, startling shades.

> *Chitralekha, Chitralekha, chitra ekhon akana. Chitrapatot chintasil ek chintanayak akana.*
> Chitralekha, Chitralekha, please draw a picture. On your canvas draw a thoughtful leader.
> *Jane jibonore rong shukula. Mane jibonore gabhi neela.*
> The people's life in color and white. The mind's life in deep blue.
> *Patra duti sajai loa. Duyoti rong milai loa.*
> Decorate the two pots. Mix the two colors.
> *Tulika tuli loana.*
> Please pick up the painting brush.
> *Eti duti rekhare, sabadhanatare*
> With one or two lines, carefully
> *nayan aka durodoroki.*
> Draw sharp-sighted eyes.
> *Onagota dinor abhinaba puwa.*
> Of days yet to come, an unprecedented morning
> *Xima aximor xima buji poa*
> Which understands the limits of the limitless.
> *Bakhya ekhon aki diya, lakhyajone lakhya powa.*
> Draw a heart so millions can reach their goal.
> *Tulika tuli loana.*

Consolatio

1.

They say *consolatio* is an old genre, and rightly so, for what is older than death, than grief? They say Seneca consoled mourners with Adam's sin, that death is ordained to humans. But what of mourners who know only Krishna, the god who never truly dies but is born again and again to save mankind?

Krishna, the boy so dark and charming, they painted him blue, playing his flute and tricks to reel in the milkmaids, the villagers, every anxious heart?

They do not say, in *consolatio*, how to move through a house in which the most magical boy has been whisked away. They do not say how to approach his oldest brother, who sits alone in a bedroom, playing a bamboo flute. They do not say how to answer the widow who hands you her son, dark and round-bellied, and says *this is the reincarnation of your cousin*. They do not say what philosophy to offer parents too Marxist to believe in religion at all, who've known wars with the British, the Bengalis, the Indian government, but whom you've never seen quite as stricken as this.

2.

The image that encircles my nine-year story is this: a boy, clearly American with his new sneakers and black suitcase and lanky limbs, hunched on an airport chair. That Oxomiya cloth, the red-and-white bordered gamoosa, was draped around his neck, as it is done warmly for all *good mornings*, all *goodbyes*. He was sobbing into the embroidered end, his face hidden from his relatives, who circled him, wordless.

3.

The last event my cousin photographed with his family was Diwali, that pan-Indian Hindu festival of lights. In the photos, he had alighted sakis on a banana tree someone had brought into the courtyard. There he stood, on the very side of that courtyard where, weeks later, his body would be bagged. He smiled before a tier of lights that promised to call Lakshmi, the open-armed goddess of wealth who sits upon a lotus, before elephants who shower the land with coins.

It was with my cousin's camera that I photographed the one-month rite commemorating his passing. It was through the lens he once used that I saw his family gathered in two rows under a yellow canopy, to listen to the townspeople who had come to read the Geeta. Strangely, it wasn't a dismal affair: the day was fresh and bright, the yellow canopy filtering swaths of light, even through the smoke. Everyone wore light cotton clothes, styled in the simple Sankari way, and the middle sister-in-law had wrapped her own mekhla around me. The bhokot, a shiny-faced man who looked much younger than seventy, read passages I couldn't follow — but his rhythm was measured, as if reading a poem, and every now and then he paused to ask the audience a question. Folks answered openly, even joked, and a yellow butterfly flitted all afternoon between ground and canopy, between canopy and sky.

My uncle, that old Marxist, stood off to the side, and I rose beside him to photograph the scene: women sifting the raw rice and chickpeas for Prasad, smoke rising from chips in a low stand, my cousin's wife, his mother, the bhokot in a tier of anxious faces. Still, I couldn't photograph some things: my uncle, that old Marxist, who stood off to the side, all of us prostrating at the end of the courtyard, where the body had not been, even my uncle kneeling in prayer. And that yellow butterfly on that strangely peaceful day, flitting between ground and canopy, between canopy and sky.

4.

I am angry that it took me nine years to return, and that I will never see you again in this fucked state of affairs. I am angry that you ate yourself to death, and left us too shaken to read the body you left. I am angry that there was no one to treat you when your heart seized, that being in the wrong place at the wrong time helped kill you. I am angry at all the policies, all the histories that dictated you would die early in an outpost of an outpost. I am angry that, given the insurgency and corruption in the Northeast, we cannot be certain it wasn't foul play. I am angry that I had to hold, one by one, your weeping family in my arms. Your mother who has my father's face. Your father who outlived the zamindars but may not outlive this. Your stunned widow who handed me your son in the courtyard. Your sister who said over and over, I can't believe I'll never see him again.

I am angry that I ever imagined you would escape the ruthlessness of circumstance, that instead, I am writing this. I am angry that you were not there, slight and dark and glossy-eyed behind the glass of Lokhinath Bordoloi Airport, waiting for me. All those trips across continents and you were always, always there. I am angry that I cannot chew you out again for a joke or cricket ball gone too far, resent you for preferring my sister to me — things that were my right as your *bhonti*, what you yourself called me. I am angry that I could not say *good morning*, as I did to everyone on this *good bye* trip, to you who were the most promising of the house. The one who got to leave Assam, the one who chose to go back, the one who had had many choices. I am angry, I am angry, and there you are in the bamboo reed in the shed. You who will be given back to the Ganga, and neither my belly fire nor anyone else's can retrieve you from time or pump back your blood or spark you up to us, whole and sure of a boy.

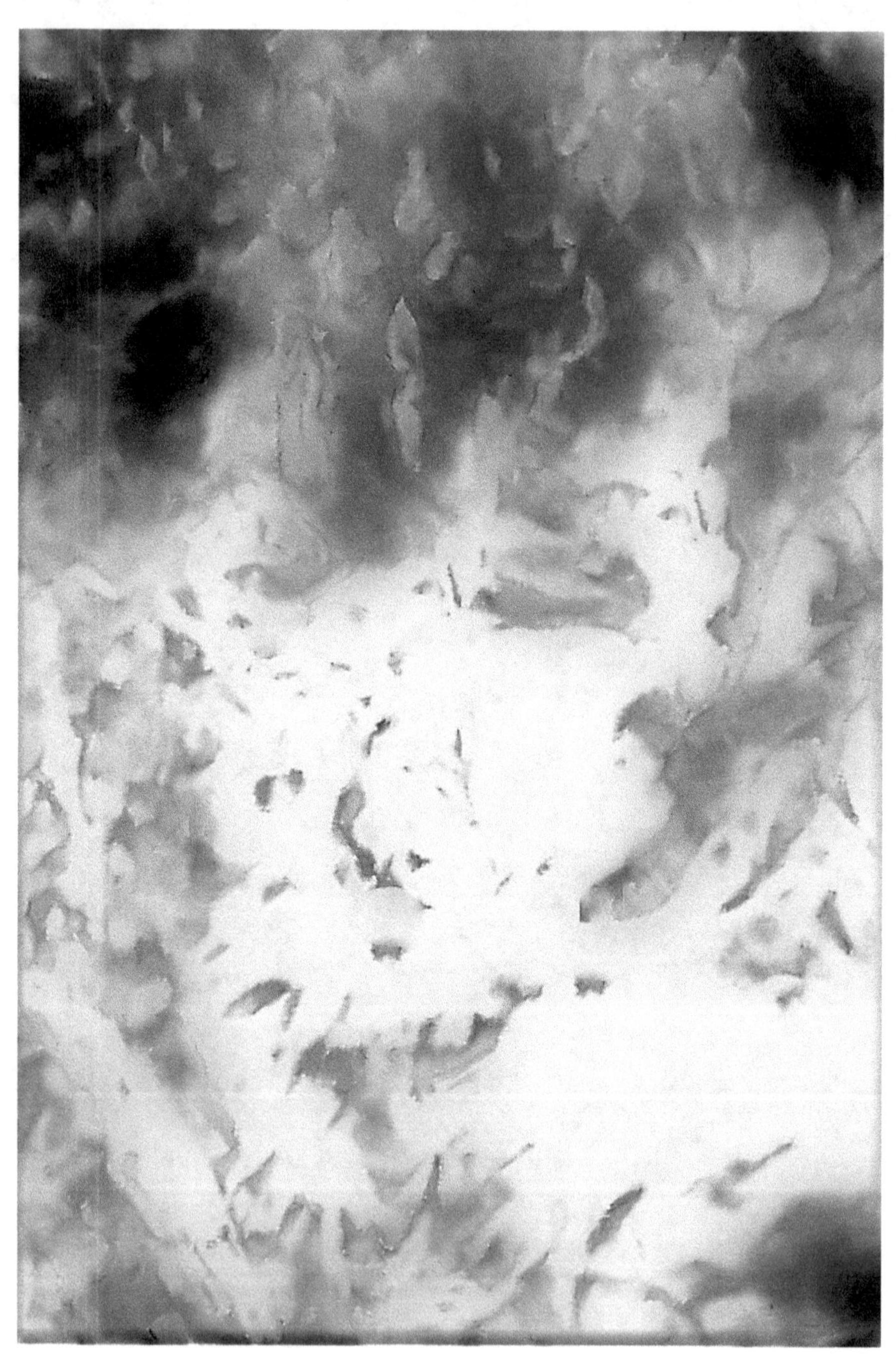

MOHAWK / MARK HURTUBISE

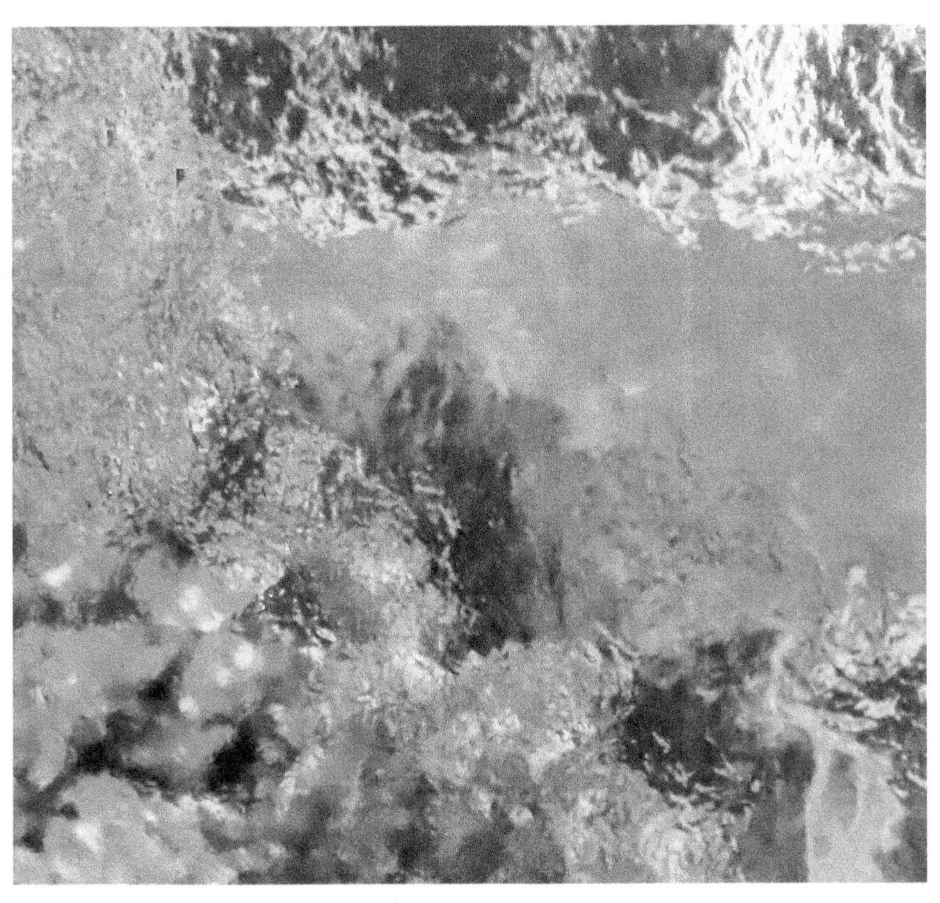

TREES / MARK HURTUBISE

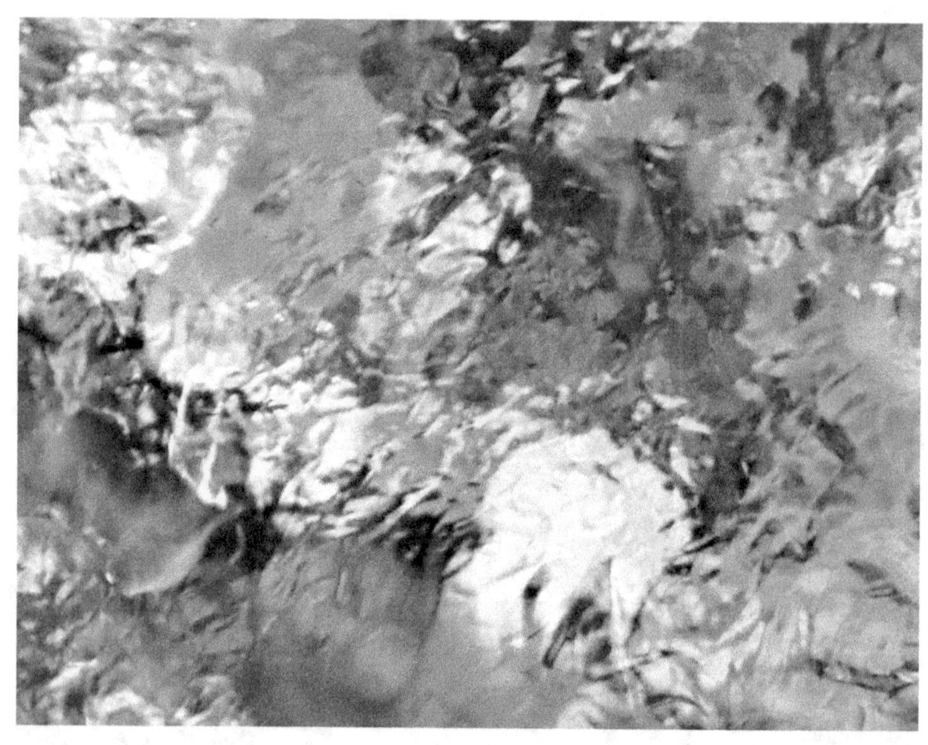

Petting Zoo / Mark Hurtubise

Bed Move

Liam Keller

There had been a rumour that Enroy's bed moved in the night. That was all. Enroy went to sleep to one side of his unclean and sort of dark and generally disagreeable bedroom and woke up on the other. Like, it was unmistakable. His bed had moved at least eight or ten feet to where it blocked his door, as if he'd barricaded himself in, and his nose was practically jammed up against the brass knob when his eyelids shot open that a.m. and it was just unmistakable. Roommates heard not a thing. That was all at first.

It's important you know about Enroy though, he doesn't tell tales. Doesn't make that stuff up. He's a depressingly truthful person. I'm not sure Enroy knows how to invent whatsoever, and if he tried he'd be terrifically bad at it. It's unthinkable Enroy could render the story he rendered about the, just, abject horror of waking with his bed to the wrong unpleasant side of his sort of dim room and his nose being jammed up to brass, the smell of brass utterly suffusing his nostrils first thing as his eyelids flashed open and registered the wrongness of his entire situation. To render such a tale, for Enroy to manage it so earnestly, so endearingly, to spin such a genuinely unsettling yarn, would be more *off* by itself than any nighttime bed-moving could be, ever, and I personally and many others would be perturbed. As soon as I heard Enroy himself vouch for the rumor, that was all for me. Besides, Enroy was only the first.

Hallewell Academy is many great slabs of dreary stone. It is coated in ivy like rivulets defacing a huge plate of melting ice or snakes crossing over one another. The silver maples that line Hallewell's imposing, north-facing front gates have a tendency to whisper at you from overhead in the fall. There is a sense of something namelessly old, and unfriendly, and possibly dangerous that hangs about the place and its narrow halls. There is a sense of something clinging to your back as you walk. It rains or snows perpetually, like the sky is spitting on you for being here, and yet something abstract holds you in place, and the grounds have a harsh, uncommon beauty to them.

This is an academy where we ski. There are the alpine skiers and the Nordic skiers, who are generally considered vaguely lower and when possible not considered at all by the Alps. Enroy is a Nord. There is academics, too, of course, interspersed between athletics. I am also a Nord, but I was an Alp before and I think that's caused a stir. Switching sides isn't so much a bad thing as it's confusing and an apparent step backwards. But I just found I liked the flats. I just developed a dramatic fear of falling down on an incline. I simply got tired of sitting on the chairlift up Collingwood Mountain and staring at, two thirds of the way up, the same rusty disfigured cedar tree I'd picked out specifically to stare at and that never died no matter how much I willed it to or thought it might. I'll be sick of the flats soon, too, and I'm definitely sick of the whole business of things moving inexplicably, and I guess I'll drop out of Hallewell before long.

The second business had to do with what they call the Top Shack, on Collingwood Mountain. The Top Shack is an unimpressive wooden structure next to the clearing on top of Collingwood where the main lift deposits skiers, and where unsavoury things are known to be done on nights off between Alps, events that cause the Faculty to purse its lips and pretend it hasn't heard a *thing* while maintaining disapproval, somehow. The Top Shack is no man's land. It's an unhinged and sort of lawless area.

On February 14, Valentine's Day, last week, the Top Shack lost its floor. The event was disconcerting and not whatsoever romantic because it essentially made the little space unlivable and encouraged clothing to be layered on rather than stripped off, given how nastily cold it was now.

I'm relating things strictly as they went down: the Top Shack lost its floor. No one could say where the floor went—when Jonathan Lockhart and Ben Almoznino were deposited first by the chairlift on the 14th and wandered into the Top Shack probably to share a joint before plunging down the mountain, the floor was absent. Gone without a trace. That students could have pulled off something like that was inconceivable. Just the previous afternoon there had been people inside the Top Shack, people who confirmed vehemently and independently the presence of a floor. The

Faculty declared with glee the building's structural integrity had been compromised and cordoned it off by noon. It was a Saturday, meaning it had been a Friday yesterday, presumably when the floor vanished, and also the 13th day of the month. Which really gave people the willies.

I was talking with Mallory Goff last Tuesday. The two of us made up one of three groups remaining in the caf this late past one in the afternoon, the caf which was filled with dull wintry light that had arranged itself in oblong patterns across linoleum. Mallory is an Alp. "What will I talk to Mirrie about?" she pleaded with me, as if I were forcing her to interact with Mirrie. She made a gross face. "Pop culture?" The words practically dropped from her mouth to the floor like stones.

"Mirrie has the face of a stork," I said, meanly. I have to be mean around Mallory Goff or else she won't take me seriously. I'm very conscious of these things. As it stands I am very mean and she takes me perhaps more seriously than anyone else.

Mallory giggled. She said, "Mirrie knows forty-seven words and has run out of possible arrangements for them. I heard her repeat the same sentence four times yesterday."

I considered this seriously. I thought of which forty-seven I might choose.

"If you only knew forty-seven words, which would you choose?"

Mallory scoffed. The question didn't seem to interest her at all. "I wonder," she said. She sort of picked at the remains of her Greek salad. I mused silently on the consequences of choosing just four-syllable words.

"So what's with the lower gym equipment?" she asked, after the silence had stretched out and started to get boring.

"Hmm?"

The shift was immediate: Mallory's eyes widened visibly and there was suddenly an excited tension between us. "You haven't *heard*?" That I hadn't heard was a fact she clearly relished. But I didn't care much and shrugged. "The lower gym equipment," she said, and her eyelids lowered to frame something like malice playing beneath them, but something innocent too, a medley of things in the blue eyes like jewels that Mallory Goff possessed effortlessly, "the treadmills and everything, not just the weights, it's all in Boucher's classroom."

And I felt, very slightly, like shy hands in a classroom, the hairs on my arms raising.

I confirmed it later. Boucher, who taught French, had entered his classroom earlier that day to find his world, the world he inhabited for so many of his daylight hours, upended. Formerly tidy rows of desks had been displaced and in their wake was equipment from the lower gym. The rowers and kettlebells and racks and cages, et cetera, the weight plates, everything, had been arranged into an utterly neat and interlocking spectacle that maximized use of space and demonstrated, it was hypothesized, something obscure. It couldn't quite be said what was being demonstrated, but the event went beyond pure chaos. There was something being said here. The equipment arranged so delicately, balanced so deftly, nothing so much as scratched, the precision and utility of the act—it took hours to disassemble—like a complex puzzle that had been expertly made up. The whole arrangement of it formed an almost perfect cube, I heard. There was a message in there surely.

The desks are gone. They have yet to be found.

It was the next day that Hallewell was stormed on and I got caught in the snow walking home with Marlon Nabi from dryland training in the lower gym, which by then had regained most of its equipment. The flakes were so fat and fell so heavily that I was sure they'd overwhelmed me to an extent. I was no longer working through them; they worked through me. The snow was not an obstacle through which I had to make my way home. I was an obstacle to be struck down by the snow in its unvarying drive to the earth.

Marlon and I pushed ahead in silence, our labor focused and grim. I remember lifting my eyes briefly at front campus, glimpsing neo-gothic hints of the Hadfield building ahead, all frigid towers and its huge clock like an eye, its arches like raised eyebrows conveying judgement. I remember thinking how truly beautiful the fog of snow was. The silence it had bestowed.

And when I arrived to my dorm, wet and sullen, I found the first note. Slipped under my door. Without a name, paper with only three words scrawled childishly on it:

You're like me.

This morning I am speaking with Marlon Nabi in the back of Calc I. We're supposed to be learning to integrate but I've already written that off. I've asked every person I know over the age of thirty when he or she last integrated something manually, by hand, and not one of them could give me a date.

Marlon is back on about the lower gym equipment. The Faculty, tight-lipped as of yet, will finally face these strange happenings head-on: there will be an official address next period in the auditorium. Something has to be said. But I already know the line they'll take; students are to blame. What else could they say? I hear Marlon mention something about Who do I think is behind it, just now. I grab him physically by the shoulders and shake him, and say, too loudly, "Don't you see, man? It's not some prank. It *can't be!*"

I really believe that. Marlon is shocked for a moment, but then breaks into a grin and takes it as a bit of theatrical hyperbole. He takes it as a joke. My being grandiose for his benefit. Parsons, our teacher, from the front, tells me to sew my lips shut and discard the notion of ever undoing that act, in more or less words.

After class we glide down long busy hallways to the auditorium and I watch my feet landing one at a time, again and again, on dull, speckled vinyl flooring designed for thousands of feet to trample it every day. I've decided after some thought to stay quiet about last night's note, slipped under my door. I'd woken uneasily this morning, thrown on a black Cranberries t-shirt and jeans, slipped into the bathroom I share with three others. There I'd splashed water on and regarded my face in the mirror. A bit red-eyed. But at breakfast no one seemed to notice. I couldn't bear to bring up the note, for whatever reason.

As we walk the halls now as a class, I think of it again. You're like me.

Then I am seated. The auditorium is large and cool and fills impassively, as with a tipped hourglass being fed sand. Students chatter in groups as they drift by. Nabi is to my left; to my right was an empty seat until just two moments ago when Mallory Goff spotted me and wound her way here to fill it. She's chewing spearmint gum. "Zombie" has been going in my head all morning because of this tee that I'm by now wearing under my collared white shirt, covertly, because we can't wear tees during school hours, we must all wear the same clothing, and I'm beginning to sweat a little, almost imperceptibly.

Then someone is addressing us, all 300 of us or nearly. It's Larsen, an actual Norwegian who is hilariously (people agree) an Alp and not a Nord, and who is also vice president at Hallewell. Larsen is saying something but I can barely understand it. I have the strangest sense of lying underwater, in a shallow kind of pool and looking up toward the sun, someone standing before it, blocking it slightly and looking back down at me. A couple bubbles escape my mouth and fly zanily to the surface. I smell spearmint.

And then we are in English. Benhabib. *A Clockwork Orange*. Benhabib is facing us and is leaned back against her desk, providing a pretty casual air, but ultimately she retains the innate authority lent by a height advantage, her being upright and the rest of us seated in tidy rows facing her and looking, for the most part, up.

"But could we say that Alex is truly good? He had no option to be good; he was forced. He was made to be good. And what are the consequences of that?" Benhabib points one lethargic digit in the direction of Tremblay, who blinks incredulously. "They," Tremblay begins but fades off. Then he declares, "No one is safe."

"What do you mean by that?"

"If they can do that to Alex, they can do it to anyone. He's just an example."

Benhabib wears what appears to be not one, but two cardigans, the one over the other, and is visibly perspiring. She says, straightening slightly, "But Alex was a criminal. If you're not a criminal, you've got nothing to worry about. Right?"

But this proves beyond Tremblay's improvisational dexterity and he just shrugs. Then he laughs a little under her continued gaze. "I guess."

Benhabib's apparently voluntary decision to dress herself in multiple cardigans is baffling and climatically inappropriate. No one else seems to have noticed. She is looking right at me now; she says my name and I keep my composure. Although, I'm jiggling one leg and it's causing my desk to vibrate—nervous habit. "What about you?" she says. "What do you think?"

I feel, very suddenly, a revulsion for my surroundings. Everything about the setting is all at once abhorrent to me; the order in every dimension. Us, an even twenty students, uniformed and hair combed, arranged so meticulously in four rows of five and Benhabib, perched on her desk now and facing us down with such flawless symmetry. That's it maybe, the symmetry of the scene. I almost can't take it. I want to pick the class up in its entirety and shake it, I want us to fly from wall to wall and cry out and kick chairs aside and flip tables and kill that pulselessness. Manically, violently untuck our shirts. I want to smile like a shark.

The words seem to arrive fully formed. I don't even have to create them; they've always been there. They propel themselves from me.

"They took his humanity when they cut the evil out of him. They flayed him and coated him in rubber. It makes me sick. Evil is a facet of humanity. Would you choose to be evil, or inhuman?" People are looking, mildly interested. Something in the tone of my voice, the word *sick*. I say: "I would rather be evil."

At the back of the class, somebody giggles.

Later, I swallow cold water in huge gulps. I can't recall the last time I had water; I just forget. I'm feeling very weird. I'm so horribly thirsty. I'm leaned against the raised wall panels of Gersham Residence's west wing hallway, which are of oak and are stained dark old, wealthy shades. I can hear the polished and echoing click of someone's shoes very far down the hall, but I can't see anyone else. It's curiously empty here. I've never seen it so empty.

There's something I need to do. But I don't know what.

I wake up the next morning on my hardwood floor and still in my jeans, with muddy boots by my bedroom door, under which the second note has been slipped. I'm wearing a Sonic Youth t-shirt. I sit up groggily and grind the palms of my hands into my eyes and retrieve the note. It's a bare minimum thing once again: no address, no greeting, only scrawled words on a plain, lined sheet of paper. The thing is folded in half diagonally. It's very eerie, actually, that fold, because no one folds paper that way.

I read:

You're like me because you know frenzy.

You know the smothering and mundane calm. You know frenzy is a release from that. I see that you feel it. The calm isn't what's fragile. The calm isn't what's delicate, what's threatened. The frenzy is threatened, always gasping for air, fighting against the thick deadening quilt of harmony, of logic, of tidiness and rules and symmetry thrown over it, that tries endlessly to kill it at birth.

Be frenzied, brim with purpose, be utterly absorbed in the moment, exist from instant to instant, as you are meant to. Feel ecstasy.

Frenzy is creation that must be created. A circle.

As I fold the note back along its diagonal and stand, finally, I notice I am no longer myself. I am slightly removed from myself. Do you know the feeling of being beside yourself? That's where I am, a little to the side, still tethered to my physical self in a funny way but no longer in total control of him. I am only a viewer. And it isn't funny, really, it's actually horrifying. Because I know there will be repercussions for the actions of my body, surely there will be, though I'm no longer totally in control of them.

I can hear excitement outside my door. Running, raised voices. Heavy steps flowing down my unit's hallway, all in one direction, mad, weird scuffling. I hear someone yell in a tone I've never heard, something almost like joy and terror together, from someone still deciding which to choose, "No it's floating. Like, hovering. It's literally fucking impossible. It's literally-" Then they've run past my door too and their voice is lost. It sounds like bulls going by. A scared herd. A parade.

I burst through my door—or I see myself do it, from the side, and I understand I've done it—and grab Enroy by the shoulders, arrest his intense motion, give him a good shake.

"Kid, what is it?" I practically scream at him. Something is making me exceptionally nervous here. Something even beyond the situation itself, which is strange at least.

Enroy is wild-eyed like I've never seen him. "Hadfield," he says to me, and I know he's incapable of lying, "it's in the air! It's *floating*."

I try to respond but only gape like a dying fish, and in a second Enroy has wriggled free from my grasp and resumed his sprint, and there are others flying past me too, fully running. It's not hard for me to follow the crowd. Though I do so more slowly. Timidly, almost.

I follow the crowd down this hallway, and then down two flights of stairs. I follow it through the reception of my residence, where the receptionist is absent although that's almost never the case. I feel the excitement of the others rushing past me and carrying me forward in huge waves, building my own anxiety until I think I might collapse.

I am outside now. It's late February and bitingly cold. I have on no coat; none of the bodies passing me seem to in fact. No one appears to notice the cold. My boots leave dirty imprints in the white below them. I am following those other bodies down Moore Street and then onto College, and through Kensington Park onto Back Campus, which looks ugly in this light, ravaged by three-hundred crisscrossing sets of tracks. Snow churned up.

Front Campus is worse, when I reach it. It looks like it's been dug up. In fact, the snow is barely there, replaced by slushy mud, one grotesque brown pool. But that's not what draws the eye.

It seems every student at Hallewell has arrived here and has stopped. Together we've formed an approximate ring around Front Campus, depositing ourselves in mismatched, shambly groups. A few of us stand alone—I do. And above us, thirty feet above, maybe, quivering slightly as though held delicately between a massive, invisible forefinger and thumb, is the Hadfield building. There's no reason for it to be there, so high over us, when it's never been there before. And yet.

It's as though Hadfield gazes at us, at me, and it looks like it might drop at any instant but doesn't. It isn't only students here; everyone is here. The huge building's arches of time-darkened stone are somehow more pointed now and somehow meaner than they ever were, and it's looking at me. I drop my eyes and look down to my boots, which are still caked with mud.

I notice my apprehension is gone. I feel a sudden calm. I look at the mud around me, the slush and the filth of it all, for a long time and I barely feel the cold.

I have the strangest sense that I'm being watched.

But that can't be. Every face is riveted to the grotesque floating display that looms over us like a seam in reality come undone. Every expression is dumb, or giddy, or scared. Hundreds of cheeks pink from the wind and every chin, every one, is tilted up. And mine too; now I'm looking up, no longer at my boots. From the side, I've been watching the body I would normally inhabit and I've seen myself look up. Only, I'm not looking at the display as those others are. I'm looking past it and to the sky and something serene is happening to me.

It's just the sky is blue like I've never seen, and it's crisp, like a sheet that's been plucked from the line and spread deftly and tucked so evenly and severely the idea of a fault, even, a wrinkle, is unthinkable. And I know that spring is coming soon. It's just around the corner. The chattering and hushed voices around me falls back like I'm on a conveyor sliding away from it all. I have a feeling like spring as I breath in and fill my lungs to their maximum and I almost can't bear it. The cold is utterly absent. I feel, suddenly, the infinity of this single moment.

And I almost go to pieces, with the ecstasy of it all. Just something about it.

Tokyo, 2017, from the Encounter With Self Series / William Lewis Winston

In Flight — Dublin, 2019, from the Encounter With Self Series

/ William Lewis Winston

Angel, Kanazawa 2017

/ William Lewis Winston

Two Sikhs, Agra Train Station 2015

/ William Lewis Winston

Buddha Blesses LA

Jon Cohen

Inception 2022 Finalist

It arrives out of nowhere, as certain as smog and the tiny Lakers flags that pop up in SUV windows when the team makes the Finals: The Buddhist bracelet with its polished tiger eye, turquoise, and forbidden lava rock beads.

How did this spartan jewelry end up on the wrists of Hollywood power brokers and balding executives across Los Angeles, replacing gold Daytonas and Pepsi Submariner Rolexes?

One bracelet, three bracelets, does one wear them on both wrists? Why the fuck not?

Some say a great wind blew in from Tulum, Mexico to Los Angeles, a sirocco of positive vibes whipped up from a yoga summit, fueled by Ecstasy and Molly, and small-batch Tequila. Was the Buddhist jewelry a recent improvement on those fabric wristlets that Mexican street vendors and expats weave together from colorful thread that summarily fall apart in ocean water? Perhaps the more durable bracelet originated in Tibet.

In the end, does it really matter? Does *anything*? Buddha would plainly say "no." The vibe in L.A. has gone from relaxed, to terribly relaxed, Buddha might even say "complacent." If a string of polished beads infiltrates this crazy world, one region at a time, who should question the reason why?

Certainly not Pharaoh Goldberg, the doe-eyed Hollywood actor from New Jersey, son of a renowned tri-state orthodontist and an eighties supermodel. As the hottest property on the market, Pharaoh openly eschews his fame.

Day at the Park / Joy Kloman

Inception 2022 Finalist

Carnal Conversations

Cynthia Close

Inception 2022 Finalist

"The new art will be an art where everything is ground up, mixed up, broken up, piled up, scratched, hacked up and blown up. Everything will be used to create art: the complete furnishings of a room, stoves, tables, beds, chests, scraps of cloth, padding in short everything will be used and mixed up pell-mell . . ."
Otto Mühl, November, 1961

Richard said my first post should be written when I'm drunk. Reminds me of the day he put a lined notebook with a Harvard U. logo on the cover and a pen in my hand twenty years ago and said, "write" or the day in my studio after a very satisfying evening in bed when he asked why I never use green in my paintings. Now I'm a grandmother. Then I was a mother, but the daughter part of me causes the most distress. My mother is still alive. I'm one of those workingwomen in the middle. I knew my great-grandmother; she died on my 14th birthday. She was an only child. My grandmother, born in 1900, was an only child. My mother was an only child. I'm almost an only child, my daughter is an only child, and now her first born (she tells me she wants one more) is a girl. This genetic pattern may or may not hold any scientifically objective significance, but what Richard jokingly calls my "*irrational self-confidence*" in being female is deeply rooted in the past.

HENRICUS

CRISTINA BRYAN

INCEPTION 2022 FINALIST

"You are bone idle," my mother-in-law Mrs. Perrotts remarked when I arrived home from work one Saturday evening shortly before Christmas. The night was cold, and the paving stones were slick with filth and frost.

Mrs. Perrotts had been pretending to sleep. "Been at the tavern?" she croaked.

"Nay, Mrs. Perrotts." I comforted myself by picturing her false ginger hair on fire. I went into the kitchen and didn't come out.

This was a few weeks before I left the town of Oxford to dwell among wild Savages.

John Perrotts and I had been servants at the college Saint Edmund Hall, and had dwelt quite happily there for three years without having to see Mrs. Perrotts once. My John had died at Michaelmas of the bloody flux. Mrs. Perrotts arrived the day of the burial. She simply said she was tired of living in the country. She set herself up in the bedchamber, letting me make do with the rush pallet in the kitchen.

I want to point out at once that I'd learned how to read, write, and do calculations when I was a child. This is simply to say that unlike other servants I was raised for better things. But I didn't object to my college work, which involved cleaning and laundering. The six Saint Edmund Hall masters were quiet and kind and their dwellings in the college not far from my own.

This was in the year 1608. I don't know what the year is now, so don't ask.

The Last Storm / Jeanne Wilkinson

Inception 2022 Runner-up

MORGAN

RON PULLINS

INCEPTION 2022 RUNNER-UP

Our man wakens and finds the world has stopped. Zero at the bone. A sudden, unexpected, deadly kind of silence has wakened him. Everything has changed. The world has altered.

Our man pulls the sheet up to his nose, stares at the ceiling. A winter morning. At early dawn.

Today will be another day of catastrophe. Again, another day.

Things must return to normal. Our man peers out, over frost that has crept up his bedroom window, sees snow outside. The bedroom is cold.

Our man must — again — throw off the sheets and push himself into the day. Yes, he must. He must get to his coffee.

Our man toggles the switch; the lamp doesn't work. He tries again; it fails again. The overhead isn't working. The clock by his bed has stopped. He no longer hears the fridge on the floor below. The furnace in the basement, the clang of steam pipes, all have fallen silent.

The power's off. That's one thing, and it's dangerous, different.

How have such things occurred? How have things happened? Who's allowing this to be the way things are? And what changes will all these changes bring to him? Which is all that is important. Most important. Being, as he is, at the center of the universe. Of course he is. Aren't we all?

Perhaps something from outside has entered his zone, corrupted the mechanism of his being, disturbed the operation of his now.

RUST / RYKER WOODWARD

INCEPTION 2022 WINNER

Debutante's Ball / George L Stein

Goldilocks Zone 2022 Finalist

Sunflowers in Soup

Xiaoqiu Qiu

Goldilocks Zone 2022 Finalist

"Kveld lifir maðr ekki
Eptir kvið norna."
("A man does not live a single evening
After the decree of the fates.") — Poetic Edda

In that moment, you're
naked: it did not
present, but disguise
Strokes
after color-
ful strokes, it is always
half and more
than what it stems:
the dying cannot commiserate
the guilt of the dead;
they have their own decay, petal
after petal, to hide behind.
only in the rich, spontaneous cata-
strophe, death becomes meta-
phoric, the tawny seed beds discharge
A dark remorse
of the kneeling figure: the vividness
of it, the dying laid level
with the dead, the discoloring backdrops—

this has always been the painting
Every day, when death comes
with its pre-sketched yellow edges, you
the leaf that grows beside
it, no less bright and full enough
to fall.

ASSISI

WILLIAM LEWIS WINSTON

GOLDILOCKS ZONE 2022 FINALIST

Last Sunday morning as the shuttered light
began to work its way between the slats and find
a path across the floor and down the
steps, their long flight into the underworld,

where first was thought the rough stones from the
valley would suffice to quiet there and make a small
place worth staying for a while, worth contemplation
of a sort that men with weapons, crowns and holy books

would not notice in their haste to raise a room above
and then another and a tower, too, and then atop that a
symbol of what they had done, glowing, so it could be
seen from far, in battle and in night and storm,

Francesco stirred from centuries without the keys or need
of them, as he always does on days like this, and stretched and
rose and took a walk around the vast halls under the domes,
glittering with gold and glass as if they could capture

light, some new species hemmed around the edges, and among
the thick columns vaulting into measured branches — so
unlike the real light and the trees always waiting on the
hillsides outside the town and down by the river,

where he was headed for a breath of fresh air and birdsong and
his usual slow dance among the mists to remind him of
something he never could remember, and
where no one would be to ask him.

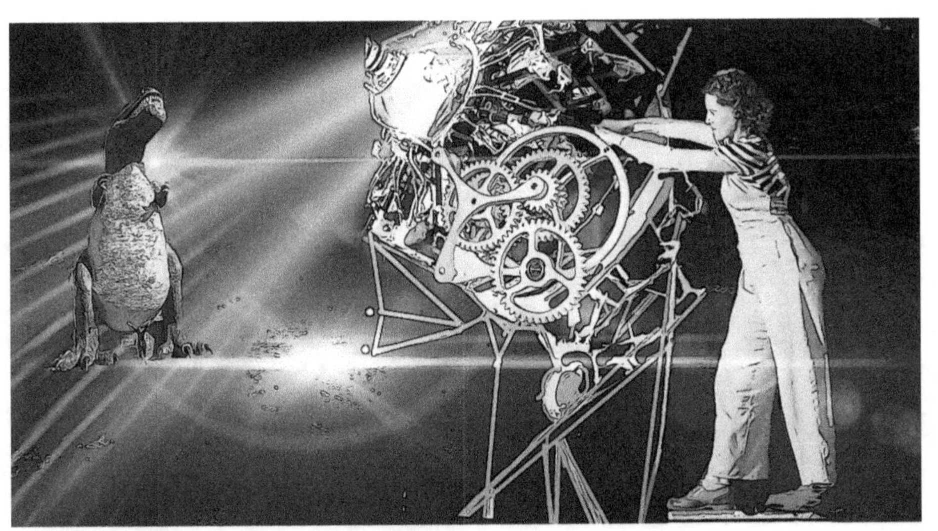

Chasing Chester / Deborah McMillion

Goldilocks Zone 2022 Finalist

THE WEIGHT

WILLIAM LEWIS WINSTON

GOLDILOCKS ZONE 2022 FINALIST

I say I would not have
cast the stone, entered the room,
fled the scene, hidden the lie, or
stolen the loaf of bread,
would not have let go the terrible secret, or
taken up arms, crawled from the trench,
would not have crossed the line, and that
I would not have given-up the names. Or
I would have done it all — in either case
a presumption of the pure, the holier-than-thou,
the dogma, the denunciation,
the intention and the pretty design. But
no matter the weight,
tests sit out of reach in a lost past,
judgment fails, and accidents of existence
unfold in places, times or wombs, in
transmigrated souls gone awry,
sensibilities gained, rebuked or blind
not by agency or choice but by
encounter, chance or fortune,
a trip, a fall or an impossible rise—
when nothing is so certain,
no depth of field so secure as not to
dissolve in a moment into its opposite.

SWELLING

RAÏSSA SIMONE

GOLDILOCKS ZONE 2022 RUNNER-UP

Tell me that you love my feral hair
Again
That you are unlike the boys who would gamble me for a seashell or who would
Coax my mouth open when their wanting ruptures

Why can I not be watched
As steady and honest as rain?
Will you witness me for a little while, dear,
Hold a grandfather clock heart until it is too heavy
Or until the
Golden momentary variation in voltage between us lapses and
Out from your teeth will come downcast words of boredom or
A tickle to flee
And I will
Nod and likely look to the lake and hold myself to its chilled promise

You can tell the water anything.

Little Box

Kendal McGinnis

Goldilocks Zone 2022 Runner-up

You spend your time after the funeral picking up your life and saying good-bye to it. You do the kinds of jobs that men who give you unsolicited advice say will make you interesting later. So you're in Concord, Massachusetts wearing an orange vest and a walkie and non-slip shoes with steel toes going around saying Mel do you copy and Mel says yes I copy. People have big ideas now. Mel included. TikTok speaks to Neoliberalism so she has the term and can give a small Ted Talk on American puritanical values and how we're all imperialists who fashion ourselves the underdog but no one's going to mention you or how you're in non-slip shoes and an orange vest walking around going Mel do you copy.

Mel's an encyclopedia on juice. She can tell you about the dawn of the company's foundation, where the grapes come from, its exhibition at the Chicago World Fair in 1893. But she's embarrassed by Concord. The city layout is as mundane as any other New England town, a McDonald's, a Starbucks, a stoplight with hanging telephone wires, a spider-webbed Best Western along the expressway. But Concord is a family of lazy settlers. Twenty minutes by car from Plymouth Rock. No one's ancestors or posterity here ever manifest destiny-ing. It's just the spot to live and die.

Anybody, says Mel, can go on Google and search what it is to be a working-class American. Mel says this in big hoorahs through several layers of personal protection equipment. But no one will mention what it feels like to bend over and fixture a gasket between a pipe and valve and pump juice from the tank in cellar nine to the tank in the backlot. That is for sure. Just wait thirty-six years. The vest and the walkie'll become you. The big black shoes, the Levis, you'd never guess we're not all dykes here laughs Mel a hearty jostling sort of laugh. Oh boohoo, don't fret, it's not homophobia, it's just that defense mechanism that saves from waning and aging femininity, something to do with the working-class thing, we'll circle back. You'll hear a variation of this joke another hundred times anyway by the end of the harvest. Let's be clear, you're making the nonalcoholic alternative to wine. A drink for churchgoers, people with good American values.

Taking to heart unsolicited advice from men becomes a quirky part of your personality. You'll see later. These men are more or less a demographic. They think you're funny when other people think you are too quiet or too crude. You remind them — but of course not too much — of their own daughters. They save you. They take you under their wing. You have a landlord in Leadville, Colorado, where you do another one of the jobs that are beside the point, that takes you out one night and buys you bratwursts at a brewery on the town's main street which is called Main Street. Jim is his name. Three or four beers you drink together.

Jim is handsome in the groomed, cheery, recent-Colorado-property-owner kind of way. A face that says: a positive spin! — an upward spiral! His move from the West Coast has something to do with taxes and also maybe a new hunting law or a wolf sanctuary nearby — you miss that part between sips of beer and the brewery is loud and buzzing with people. No clink of ski boots or gloves being tossed on the table, none of that. It's sort of a dreamy local crowd on this night. Men who plow the runs, college boys who check your tickets, a neighborhood restaurant owner and his wife. Jim's monologuing — it's characteristic of the demographic. You've heard at this point about his divorce from Trudy, the whole thing sort of slow-burn or that's how you read it, probably he tells you too about his daughter in Humboldt County failing out of a Communications major. You notice things are weighing on him and you grab his hand. There's an intimacy between you and Jim. Something you've had before and will again with men that give advice so laudable it transcends whole generational boundaries, job markets, gender divides.

You start sleeping one day with one of these men. Craig or something. He lives in a swanky but minimalist apartment overlooking the Pulaski bridge (on the Brooklyn side, obviously). He's much older than you but jogs and stays away from red meat. His mattress and books are on the floor. The view is spectacular and the books on the floor are all ones that quirky Bushwick girls your age love: the Zadie Smiths, the Aimee Benders, the Lidia Yuknavitches. Craig is a little shamefaced about his studio. He used to work in homeland security, but his conscience gets the better of him. Now he's at a hedge fund in the city. We're all a little implicit, he whispers to you as you lean with your back against the kitchen sink, his hands gripping the counter on either side of you, maybe his thumb in one of your belt loops (in a hot way not a predatory way). In 2001 he was working in the Pentagon, he says. You try to mimic the expected jaw-drop he's after. Craig was there on the day it all happens. He doesn't ask you of course about your own 9.11 story because you would've been too young to have a personal anecdote. Mostly likely he doesn't care anyway. There's no time for that now. The fact alone that he was in the Pentagon on the day it all goes down, he's using your generation's lingo now, getting really close to your ear, it makes women want to put out for him he says. He says it coyly, sheepishly, he's using "put out" sarcastically — it's ironic, no Greenpoint hipster would use "put out" and mean it. But don't worry, he's not really a hipster, he tells you this before you get to the part where you're between his hands leaning with your back against the kitchen sink. Craig's really self-aware. He shrugs his own narrative to the side in a lionhearted act of humility. You wonder later whether you sleep with him because you too are taken by the sheer valor of his Pentagon story or whether there's a look-at-me-now moment when you're undressing in front of the floor-to-ceiling window overlooking the Pulaski bridge, the New York skyline big and bright before you, you can almost see the Chrysler building, the Empire State, the TJ's on 3rd Avenue where the organic people go to get their Trader O's, all of it.

Jim's hand is getting soggy in yours. This moment means so much to him. Big, hunky conservative men are all softies, overly sentimental. They want the troops to come home or they want the troops to stay there or they want the troops to finish their duty but what the duty is is not the duty of these big, hunky conservative men to say, no. The American flag outside his Leadville log-cabin dream home says enough, doesn't it. Jim is a good listener. It makes him feel good that you take advice from him. He's crying now, babbling a bit, he's saying something like Trudy or troops or Truist — that might be his bank — who knows. You can't tell, he's too wet and too pink. Men with fresh snow still in their beards begin looking over at you at your table, which is elevated. The seats themselves are old whiskey barrels. The bar is original, from the original German pub, but everything else has that manicured renovation feel. A high yellow-lit ceiling with wooden beams running across it. Young healthy servers from Liberal Arts backgrounds, scruffy and intellectually worn-out but from well-off families. No one's been here before, but we've all been here before. It's just someone's take on an impression of something else. The more you move the more you understand this. Every town or city has a one-dimensionality to it. When you pick up your stuff and load the car and say good-bye, the town itself folds itself flat like the turned pages of a pop-up children's book until it's just a road and then a highway — the I-5 then the I-70 then the Indiana Expressway, all in your rear window. Home is not a place, home is the men who give you unsolicited advice.

A bearded man at the table parallel to yours mouths to you: Is he okay? Jim's mom — you've gotten to the bottom of it — is married and remarried seven times before Jim turns twenty-five. Add Trudy and the loser daughter into the mix and you have a recipe for a big, hunky man to break down at the gentle touch of your hand, the snow falling in silent sheets on the sidewalk outside, the old rickety bar and a sexy modern backsplash behind him. Jim leans in, squeezes your hand tighter. The chatter dies off. The brewery blurs away. It's just his puffy pink face. You almost know it's coming and then it comes. He grabs your cheeks dramatically, spontaneously, and pulls you close. He turns your head slightly and whispers into your ear, I have a little box. Jim has a little box and it is filled to the brim with bad and negative emotions. He just puts it, he says, on the edge of a small shelf high in his office and doesn't touch it except on dark days. Put it all in the box, divorce yes daughters yes death of an old touch-football friend him too his mother's marriages yesyesyes. Put it in the box. He looks at you so piercingly you worry he's going to dive into a kiss on your lips. Where is your box, he whispers. Huh. Where do you keep your little box?

Mel invites you to dinner at her house after your shift. It's fall and the harvest at the company is ending soon. Mel lives in West Concord, by the golf course. She looks nice, she has tomorrow off. Her dress is something floral, something silky. Oh this? She'll say. Target. Mel and her ex-husband lose everything in one way or another. A second mortgage taken out on a business gone underwater. Not to the Great Recession but to a corrupt business partner who flees to Florida says Mel's new man Pat. Not tonight Mel says, giving him a look. But Pat won't let up, it's part of his own narrative now. You can't get to know him or eat dinner at their house in West Concord without hearing the whole shebang. Mel and her ex go bankrupt shortly after the evil business partner — the story's growing in melodrama, you like it. Mel divorces him as a last blow to the man's self-esteem and he dies shortly after. She meets her new man at the funeral, do you believe it? A romance out of dust and ash says Pat.

Mel serves watermelon. It's a cool orange-skied fall evening. Everything this mundane takes on meaning at a certain hour and the hour is now. The clouds seem to be going in all directions. Pat gives you one of his good beers from the refrigerator in the garage. He winks at you, like he's sharing a secret only you can be let in on. You're comfortable here in Concord, sitting on a porch with chipped paint and strung-up patio lights, the smell of something hot and baked in a dish smothered with cheddar. It smells so heavenly. Mel and Pat are laughing at each other. The conversation loses you but they're talking about money in a sort of playful way, writing off the hardship and anxiety with self-deprecation. You don't like when working-class people like you and Mel and Pat complain about cycles of poverty. It's much prettier when fluffy academics do it or you can read it in a book or something. But Mel and Pat don't matter much, they're just characters in one of your stories anyway. Not real people like your dad. The dish is eaten and you are tired and Mel is scrolling Tik Tok in the dark. There are dogs barking coming from the screen.

Your little box is in the passenger seat and you are driving. It's a boring twenty minutes from Concord to Plymouth Rock. You've settled on reverse manifest destiny. The little box and you and the long trek across the country. You park your car in the visitor center parking lot. You're expecting it to be inconsequential and graffitied in something unintelligible but it's beautiful actually. Simple and complicated and holding so much history in its body. The beach before it is gated off because it's sacred to you and your ancestors and your posterity, the ones who make it out west. You hop the gate clutching your little box tight against your chest and walk it out past the shoreline.

Craig isn't all that bad, you promise. The hugs he gives you after you buzz into his loft are big and breathy, all-encompassing. He hugs you like someone who loves your body, not for the body itself. Your dad used to hug you like that. Your dad wasn't perfect: A California transplant from Concord, Massachusetts. Came across as a reader but was totally not a reader. Made his way across America, stopping, working odd-jobs, becoming interesting. He did that thing that dads do where they compete to make their lives sound adventurous but use self-deprecating language to do it so it shows humility and he was bashfully patriarchal but also a leftist so therefore complex and he was insistent on his Mayflower story, his 9-11 story, his retirement dream home in Colorado, everything subject to embellishment but never for malice. He's the guy that poemed and syntaxed you into existence. You miss the way he hugged. He lives in a little box now on your desk in-between the mascara and the two deodorants you can't decide on.

FOR ME, FOR YOU

C. Tai Tai

Goldilocks Zone 2022 Winner

給妳

給我

Ya estoy cansada pero sigo

I am full of aphorisms seeing the reflection of light through the
G A Z E
of others

讓我說不清楚為什麼 así <u>es</u> AHORA ESTAMOS YA TRATANDO
DE SER MEJOR
MÁS ASTUTA learnt from that stern look of disapproval
已經不夠力量的時候再往前看。

ROJO 熱血的顏色 因為我沒有其他的生命來衡量
algunas veces ni siquiera me reconozco
trato de ver cada momento como una oportunidad de conectarme al
mundo más grande pero me
decepciona el mundo

TAL VEZ

si no podemos cambiar la escultura estructura,

我每個行動都得 . . .

(poem repeats from top)

Body Count

Michael Cullinane

Rigel 2023 Finalist

Despite always being the first to arrive at her Human Growth and Development class, Ivy Barlowe didn't say hi to Mr. Leith, and Mr. Leith didn't say hi to Ivy Barlowe. She would quietly choose a seat in the back at Lab Table 6, hiding behind her phone, and dreading the moment the fuckboys walked in. But on that Friday, she decided to keep her phone in her purse and consider Mr. Leith, who sat on his spinny chair, staring out a window. Even though he was like the worst teacher on the entire planet, she felt bad for him. And she wondered about his left hand, which was loosely wrapped up in gauze the way she had as a kid, pretending to be a mummy. In his other hand, he popped poppy paper to a beat like *POP! Pop-pop-pop*. He was hella messed up, and Ivy wondered what sort of secret life Mr. Leith had after he left Stevenson. Like, maybe he'd gone to a casino the night before and had some killer poker hand and put up his car and his house, but then the guy next to him won and was all like, "Sorry, boss, but I got all your shit," so Mr. Leith punched a wall.

The rest of the class lumbered in, and Sebastian Harris, aka Fuckboy Number One, arrived on time for once. Ivy couldn't help it; he made her nervous, so she pulled her phone out of her purse in case he looked at her, using the video like a mirror. Of course, no air conditioning in Room 237, so the humidity frizzed her hair out of control, and the camera angle gave her a serious double chin which she was way too young for. The room felt like one of those dusty bookstores from a movie where a kid opens a book and a crusty wizard pops out. It was literally the only room at Stevenson that hadn't been renovated when the mayor dumped all that money into the school for her photo op. Antonio, that creepy kid with the beard who looked like he was forty, posted a video on TikTok where he found a jar in the back closet that read *human foetus, 1977* with an actual human being inside like some sort of ancient pickle. And somebody had drawn a butthole with a sharpie right in the middle of the chalkboard, and Mr. Leith didn't even care enough to stick a poster over it. To Ivy, the whole thing was sort of funny but mostly depressing because having a teacher who was *that* incompetent in a classroom *that* nasty was basically criminal.

A message popped up on her phone, one of those automated ones from the school. Ivy had a meeting scheduled with her social worker Ms. Renata in the Calm Down Room. She'd forgotten. She started to stand up, but the thought of Sebastian Harris yelling, "Do you need to change your tampon?" kept her frozen. She was desperate to talk to Ms. Renata because, even though she was totally out of touch with what it meant to have a vagina in 2022, Ivy needed to vent, and Ms. Renata was seriously the only person at the school who would listen.

Only twenty-two days remained in the school year. Twenty-two days left of the hell that was Human Growth and Development. Ivy, a sophomore, didn't belong in the class. It was one of those senior electives designed to help the shitwits graduate. At the beginning of the year her counselor Mr. Huffnagle told her to wait until the tenth day to request a schedule change, but on day ten, he told her she'd waited too long. Now Ivy was seriously the only sophomore in a class of seniors who made it their mission in life to give her a nervous breakdown, which she was like super-near because of the week she'd had. Totally grounded and stuck with her mother trying to keep her busy "without getting all wrapped up in that phone of yours!" But Ivy pushed away the despair like Ms. Renata taught her because there were people suffering a lot worse, even if she didn't know a single one.

So, now, how to escape from Room 237? Ivy walked through the steps in her head. To get out of the classroom, she would have to put her backpack on and try to get Mr. Leith's attention while Lab Table 3 made creepy porno sounds. She'd try to explain that she had a pass on her phone, and she'd hold it toward Leith's face, but he'd probably just sit there with his poppy paper like, "Durr."

"Yo, bro, I think this thing is like sleeping," one of the fuckboys said. They tapped on the glass of Mr. Leith's dead hermit crab, the one serious no-

no Leith had since day one, which only made the people like Sebastian Harris and Lukas Meyers and the rest of them want to do it more because they required constant attention. But Mr. Leith didn't flinch or respond or even look at them. He just used his bandaged-up hand to itch his head like he had lice or fleas or bedbugs, and this beam of light from the window made a little halo, and Ivy could see the flakes of dandruff get scraped off his scalp. Steroids messed with guys' bodies — she didn't need Human Growth and Development to teach her that — which was probably why Mr. Leith was losing his hair, just like when she got addicted to those Hydroxycut diet pills that Bess pushed on her and she started seeing clumps of her hair in the shower drain.

All of the drama started on Tuesday when Sebastian Harris took a hit off his vape and blew the smoke into Blinky's bowl. Ivy could have yelled something like, "You're not God," but she didn't say anything, which made her feel guilty because, sure, it was just a hermit crab, but Ivy loved animals. She even thought about being a veterinarian for a while before realizing there was way too much math involved. Ivy remembered how Mr. Leith smiled when he introduced Blinky on the first day. And then he made the mistake of talking about how weightlifting saved his life and everyone laughed at him, so Mr. Leith gave up and said, "Do your assignment. It's on Google Classroom." He said it that day and every day after.

Now Blinky was dead and the fuckboys knew it and Mr. Leith knew it, but no one was doing anything about it. Like why hadn't Mr. Leith just thrown Blinky in the garbage? Jamal yelled that the hermit crab started to stink, and Bryan, who wasn't even supposed to be in the class, yelled "Stinky Blinky" and everyone laughed, including Ivy. According to Ms. Renata, Ivy suffered from impulse control issues. Laughing at sad things was the most terrible curse anyone could have, like when her mom told her that her grandfather died and she laughed. Her mom slapped her even though it was an involuntary reaction because of course she was sad as fuck because she loved her Papa.

Ms. Renata sent another message that just said "Where are you?" and Ivy almost started crying because everything felt super bottled up and ready to explode. Her motto of *I'm down for whatever* had backfired over the weekend for the hundredth time. Back in, what, sixth or seventh grade she said it to a group of boys and she saw their eyes light up like she'd just opened a bag of Skittles and invited them to *Taste the rainbow! I'm down for whatever* had some sort of power over their deepest desires. Or their dicks, which were basically the same thing. According to Ms. Renata, when Ivy said, "I'm down for whatever," she thought it gave her power, but really, Ms. Renata said, those words gave boys the right to take advantage of her and what Ivy needed were firm boundaries. Firm boundaries sounded like the same shit she'd heard every adult tell her her whole life, but when Ms. Renata said it, it sort of made sense because that woman would at least look you in the eye from time to time.

The boys from the weekend were hot and she lowkey had a crush on Georgio even before he ever talked to her. The problem was that Georgio was Shelly's crush. But as soon as he swung by McDonalds with two friends and picked up Ivy in his own car that he bought with his own money and asked what she wanted to do, and she said, "Durr, I'm down for whatever," they got that same stupid-ass look on their faces.

She didn't want to think about it, so she got her phone out and scrolled TikTok and Insta basically at the same time even though that shit is hella bad for your mental health. Like, the night before, some dork freshman DMed her on Insta and asked, *How many guys have you had sex with?* and she didn't respond, but she saw those little dots like he was typing, so Ivy waited. He thought he was real slick and wrote *100?* Then he said, *more?!?!* Then he said, *1000?* and finally she told him to shut the fuck up, and he sent back the laughing crying emoji and *Im dead,* and Ivy knew he was would post screenshots because he had absolutely nothing better to do than talk shit about her body count, which only Shelly knew because they told each other everything, which was another reason Ivy was totally freaking out.

And it was like what Ms. Bryers talked about in English class when they got hella off topic, about how there was, like, a double standard for men and women. Ms. Breyers wasn't even a feminist or trans or anything, just an old lady who read a shit-ton of books. And when they read *The Handmaid's Tale,* she talked about how things post-Trump were actually going backwards not forwards in terms of women's rights. Butterflower from TikTok said the same thing — guys fuck and girls get fucked, and guys are just pushing, pushing for it constantly. But once they have a girlfriend, they always want to know her body count, and if it's too high they get all quiet and pissed off and sulky and moody and say that they can't date a girl who isn't a virgin or close to one, so she lies and tells him she's never been with anyone or maybe just a couple people and that his dick is the biggest of them all. And it's all so pathetic because Sebastian Harris probably had a higher body count than Ivy, but when he talks about it, the guys all pat him on the butt and say "Nice job, bro!" But with Ivy, the girls talk shit behind her back and the guys talk shit in front of it.

The fuckboys started pushing the bowl on the lab table like they were playing that game where you try to see how close you can get that disk to the edge. Ivy looked up at Mr. Leith who stopped popping the poppy paper and grabbed his tongue with his thumb and index finger. She couldn't figure out what he was trying to do. Then he got something, a hair, one that fell off his balding head, and he held it up to the light and wiped it on his pants. The man was completely oblivious. Ivy figured he was sad about his hermit crab, but she didn't understand why because, even if he really loved Blinky, hermit crabs don't have identifiable personalities, and you could probably just go to the store and pay five bucks for a new one and never know the difference.

She wondered what Mr. Leith's body count was. He was, like, what? Thirty maybe. Not married because most married guys usually talked about their wives and kids, but that guy didn't talk about anything except lifting weights. So, assuming he was single and straight, and assuming he was at least thirty, he must have had sex with at least three women per year since he was eighteen. So, twelve times three. That would be at least thirty-six. His body count was probably about thirty-six.

Then Ivy began to think about other body counts, like Ms. Renata. Not to be gay or anything, but she was hot and probably constantly had guys hitting on her. Even Ivy had to turn down guys and she had hella pimples and was a little more than just a little bit overweight and couldn't afford nice clothes or anything. Guys would give their left nut for a woman like Ms. Renata. She must have given the "all access pass" at least five times a year when she got drunk or just got tired of saying no. And Ms. Renata was also like 30. That meant twelve times five. Ms. Renata's body count must have been, damn, sixty. About twice as many as Mr. Leith's. Girl fucking power.

Those idiots shoved the glass bowl again and again from all four corners of the table, and you could see the gravel and the little trees and the castle go flying around inside the bowl. Blinky was just rolling around, and the guys were laughing, and no one told them to stop because the teacher just scratched his head and popped poppy paper and the rest of the class just stared at their phones and Ivy hated all of them for being a part of a world where she literally couldn't even get up and show the teacher her pass to get out of such a toxic environment.

High school was a prison you never get to leave because even after you graduate, you still have everyone on social media calling you a slut, so when you post a picture with a guy you meet at college who is like your maybe-maybe-not boyfriend, he would be like, "Why does everyone you went to high school with call you a slut on Insta?" and he'd have hella questions about your body count and he would break up with you before you even got a relationship started.

Ms. Renata didn't understand how Ivy couldn't not be a slut. Because getting called a slut on Insta, meant you were a slut. Deleting your socials was basically impossible, so in 2022, no matter how you lived your life, your whole future was basically predetermined. Sort of like the kid who pissed his pants in class in sixth grade. In the future, when he posted a picture of himself with his wife, everyone would say, "Oh, wow, that kid who pissed his pants in Ms. Dixon's class got married."

The more she thought about it, the more she needed Ms. Renata to look her in the eye and ask her those questions like "Could you tell me more about that?" and "How does that make you feel?" because Ivy seriously just needed someone to care about her for like ten minutes because she was so tired of always putting everyone's needs ahead of hers.

Jamal pushed the bowl and Sammy cradled his hands under the lab table to catch it. The bowl slid right to the edge, and Sammy yelled, "Oh, shit," and Ivy couldn't help but laugh because the bowl was truly half on half off the lab table, like it could slip off at any second, and in a really stupid and juvenile way, hearing "Oh, shit!" really loud in a classroom is kind of funny.

Mr. Leith saw that one. He turned away from the window and put his poppy paper down, and, you could really tell that he wanted to say something, but there was some weird lump in his throat, like his Adam's Apple was all knotted up. She wanted to let Mr. Leith know she sort of cared about what was happening in his life, but that idea only made her laugh because, like, why would she care about some weird-ass dude with his armpits sweating through his polo? But maybe his life was even harder than

Ivy's. She saw Mr. Leith for one hour a day, and he was awake for like, what, sixteen hours a day. Ivy only had one-sixteenth of the picture. And, considering his pet died in that one-sixteenth, he might be dealing with sixteen problems which all piled up and left him just staring out the window like a freak. Ivy had way more than sixteen problems, but she was at least still able to talk and communicate and function in that fake-it-till-you-make-it sort of way.

It was weird to think that Mr. Leith had been in high school, which, for him, had probably been a prison, too. He seemed like the kind of guy who might have puked in gym class, not once, but all the time, which was why he went insane and built up his muscles to compensate for being a total loser who barfed every time he tried to run or make a basket. You don't look like that unless you're trying to make up for something else that's gone missing. Just like how in twenty years, Ivy would probably stare out a window, feeling all locked up, wondering what the hell went wrong.

Sammy slid the bowl, and Jamal made like he was going to catch it, but it moved too fast and tipped over and rolled like a bowling ball. The whole thing split in half, top and bottom, and gravel started coming out all over the place. They gasped and swore and Jamal stood right in the middle between the two halves which went in opposite directions. Rather than make a move to catch one, he just let both drop. One smashed before the other, you could hear that, but it was hard to tell which one smashed first, the top or the bottom, and that's the sort of thing that doesn't even really matter much because there was glass and gravel and Blinky's little toys all over the floor. Even Blinky.

The whole class looked over at Mr. Leith, and Ivy looked over at Mr. Leith. His chest was all puffed up, and his muscles were bigger than normal, and the buttons looked like they were going to pop off his sad little polo shirt. He took a super deep breath for like ten seconds, and Ivy kept thinking it was impossible to suck that much air into his lungs, but he just kept on inhaling, way past the point of normal. And what would he do with all that air? Maybe with some sort of Big Bad Wolf flex, he would just blow the entire classroom away.

The man held his breath while all the students held theirs. His nipples stuck out on his shirt like a couple of pencil erasers. He kicked the doorstop away, like, all the way away down the hall. Ivy could hear it smacking the floor like some little kid threw a block.

And the door shut.

Mr. Leith hadn't shut the door the whole year, not even when Mulligan got on the loudspeaker and announced there was a hall sweep. Seeing Sebastian Harris kill the hermit crab on Tuesday was really bad. And seeing the glass smash on the floor was awful. But that door closing was terrifying because never before in Ivy's life had she felt like she was seriously in one of those situations like you hear about on the news where some psycho trapped kids in a classroom, killing them all. Leith's eyes flashed wild, like he was part animal. He couldn't just pick out a single kid to stare down because he hated all of them. Ivy looked away, and didn't laugh, not even a little.

Ivy saw that button by the door that teachers used to call the office. Teachers used it when they were all hungover or whatever and had enough and wanted security to come. Like, "Jimmy's in the wrong seat even though he sat in the wrong seat all year, but I'm having a shitty day, so I want him GONE!" That was what the button was normally for. Ivy thought about how it might save her life. If only she could get off her stool. But students couldn't push the button. They weren't allowed.

Mr. Leith grabbed the metal garbage can next to his desk and walked over to where the bowl had smashed, right where the guys were just standing, and he squatted with a grunt and started scooping up glass with his right hand, the one without the bandage, and he flung it into the garbage can, so hard that some of it bounced out and landed back on the floor. And you could tell after about ten seconds that he was bleeding because the glass bouncing out of the garbage can was all bloody. Then the blood started dripping from his hand, and he was flinging, like actually flinging, the glass so hard that blood was seriously flying around the classroom, and the kids nearby were moving away, and a bunch of them, the girls especially, sort of huddled together by Ivy.

A drop of blood landed on Ivy's lab table and about five little tiny droplets of blood landed on her glasses, on her actual glasses.

The whole thing was so weird and so awful, and he was throwing the gravel and the little trees and the castle and everything, just flinging them into the garbage can, and it made this sort of tribal beat like, *Duh duh, smack.*

Duh duh, smack. Duh duh, smack. And then he picked up Blinky, and he sort of stopped for a second and Ivy held her breath because he was staring at his dead hermit crab which had started the whole shit show. He looked like one of those guys in an action movie who says a line like, "Now it's time for vengeance," and Ivy could tell that Mr. Leith was thinking that he needed to throw Blinky away, but he took a second to concentrate on him, maybe making some kind of tribute in his head, and then he threw Blinky right into the garbage can with another *Duh duh, smack.*

Ivy moved further to the back corner of the room. She found a tissue that she'd had in her back pocket and wiped the blood off her glasses. Getting any blood on you or your glasses was not normal. The tissue was one of those with lotion, so instead of the blood coming off, it just smeared around.

When most of the glass and gravel was in the garbage, Mr. Leith stood tall and focused his eyes on Sebastian Harris, who was just trying to lay low for a change. Ivy didn't know what Leith wanted him to do, and maybe Leith didn't even know what he wanted Sebastian Harris to do. Maybe apologize. Maybe he wished Sebastian Harris was dead.

She heard the knock at the door and she jumped, and judging by the squeals from the girls around her, half of the class shit their pants. Then she heard that cheerful voice she knew so well.

"Knockety-knock-knock!"

The door wasn't locked or anything, so Ms. Renata came in and looked around like she'd just gotten pranked. All the students were huddled in the corner of the room, and Mr. Leith was dripping blood from one hand and breathing like he'd just lost a fight, still just staring at Sebastian Harris. That woman didn't miss a beat, though, she just said, "Could I please request Ms. Ivy . . . oh, there you are. Did you forget about our appointment?"

Under her breath, Ivy whispered, "Halle-fucking-lujah." Finally, she could leave.

She already had her stuff, so she walked toward Ms. Renata who looked at her with some serious *what the fuck is going on* eyes. Ivy put her head down and got the hell out.

She knew Ms. Renata would ask her what happened, which would be annoying because living through something fucked up was bad but explaining it over and over again was even worse. But, maybe, just maybe, Ms. Renata could help Mr. Leith get better.

Ivy imagined Mr. Leith sitting on the couch in the Calm Down Room, Ms. Renata's emotional support dog Romeo weaving between his legs. Ms. Renata would ask him, "How did throwing your dead hermit crab in the garbage make you feel?" And he would probably get that same lump in his throat that Ivy got in hers when Ms. Renata asked her how something made her feel. Maybe no one ever asked Mr. Leith how he felt about anything and that was why he was so weird and losing his hair and locked in his prison.

Once Ivy's feet were out the door, she said, thank God it was Friday because she did not want to set foot in Room 237 for at least two days, if not forever.

Adrift in Deep Sea / Penny Senanarong

Rigel 2023 Finalist

Motorcycling to Mexican Time and the Zen Sea

Gregory Ormson

Rigel 2023 Finalist

Biking toward Mexico, the jagged mountains framing both sides of Arizona's Highway 85 are now in my mirror. Wind and heat push me forward to where it is not much of a leap for my Midwestern imagination to place me in a scene from an apocalyptic biker movie on a two-lane road headed into the heart of dust. At the border wall, problematic for drug mules and Americans with criminal records trying to cross, the guards peer at my shiny wheels. I'm neither criminal nor mule, but I'm wary of the gun-wielding guards; the mind-meld of television news depicting Mexico as dangerous, and at this wrecking wall I'm heating up like one of Dante's eighth-circle bolgers.

My motorcycle brothers and I cross the wall into Mexico, and our bikes are screaming to hell with America and our jobs, if we still got them, left behind us with our families — fathers, children without fathers, and desperate mothers trying to become younger in their old age. Will I ever cross the border back to America?

So this is Mexico?

There's a lot of dust.

Dust eats away at my skin. The leather I wear makes every minute an inferno on the motorcycle. Heat explodes up my ass, creeping past crack and sack to pillage my spine and overburden my shoulders. But I am an adult, I am in Mexico, I have documents and a clean record; I can drink, buy drugs, or pay to make fantasies come true. I can also do none of that or get a ticket to take the pirate ship and sail into the mystic with tourists, eating as much shrimp and drinking as much Dos Equis XX lager as I can handle.

I kept thinking I was Jack Nicholson, playing the detective in a film he never made; one around the time when he was still in his Blood and Wine prime as a jewel thief. What would fucking Jack do in this cheaply shot biker flick, us bikers as dirty subjects? Grainy video shows Jack and us approaching the wall. Nothing happened. Wasted video.

My body pumps with the rumor of life, and my mind believes in the music of the Sun; its giant scythe of blinding white light waits for us this November riding to the Sea of Cortez, its blue tint a powerful pacifier. Nearby, a peasant labors to ride an old black bicycle. He may be Don Juan from Carlos Castaneda's writings. His shrunken body leans over the handlebars, and his floppy watermelon hat riffles its brim without flying away — an agent of the apocalypse, or a lonely man cantering among the prickly saguaros? Lord, when he turns his wizened face of the sun towards me, does he know my fate? I ride on and wonder what has happened to the People of Don Juan.

Mile by mile, bare space testifies to failure, and a lot of what I see is not thriving.

My bike explodes through sand and its endless box of a hungry place where time is a mind warp not easily categorized. I lose track of it though, and my Harley-Davidson, desperate for traction, loses it on a sandy one-track road. Six times driving past my turn, but I didn't see it. None of us did, and we couldn't figure out what happened. Maybe it was a warp, and the ticking clock of blood and bone that is me — astride my Harley-Davidson — rides closer to a border we have already crossed. I daydream.

Senorita, look at my moving machine as it spits out pinecones, remnants of a once-living tree that will no longer straddle the earth. The revolutions of angst and daydreams of senoritas keep me guessing about time. Forward on the bike, I remind myself to not daydream. It's dangerous.

Once while motorcycling on a high cliff in Hawaii during fierce winds, I was daydreaming and looking at the Pacific Ocean, my front wheel spinning revolutions and gripping a thin margin of error just inches from the edge and certain death, a Don Juan moment, a voice within my voice telling me not to die.

At the Harley-Davidson Museum in Milwaukee, a CAD drawing orders the sequence of the dirty work happening below my belt: squeeze, suck, bang, and blow. A puree of gas and oxygen firing the wily explosions in the dark interstices of a Big Twin engine, just like Jack's active and lusty Id. Jack, my brothers, and I ride by faith and trust that the explosions below our belts will not blow up our balls and send us to another kingdom. Trust is necessary and underrated by bikers and actors.

Rolling again, the wheels are shredding cactus in a scene that Nicholson had written himself for his screenplay. Now he drives his black Mercedes around Studio City hoping to find a parking space in front of The Aroma Cafe. His smile, a trickster, combing his hair plugs and grinning into his rearview mirror murmuring, "I am the greatest that ever was."

The bike I drive, banging its way through the streets on the way to my cheap café, is an agent of attraction and repulsion. Everyone hears the Harley-Davidson song because it's loud. I rumble along cobblestone streets as my bike's Big Twin engine belts a song from the chrome pipes and echoes between the worn buildings.

Vendors on this Malecón, tired of filthy rich gringos and gringas, are happy for the taco money, but they don't want to look. They don't need to. They have heard every biker's sad story and see us wounded animals coming south, revving up rubber and spit in the acrid smoke of a burnout pit; loud, testosterone-fired homages to a furious Beowulf, a white man's epic angst in the motorcycle's sound and fury. Pfft, better to gather eggs from the chickens. But resistance to my bike's open-throated rumble is futile . . . they must, and they do, turn and stare: cops, street vendors, women, and men.

It's a school day and children are on the playground. A few of them run to the iron gate barring entry from the road. They smile at the leather-clad gringo and wave. He waves back. Washing over him, a tinge of regret thinking back to his school days.

Don Juan is now far behind, and I swerve to avoid a dog chasing its tail like a dust devil. Next to the wispy devil, a boy is holding a watermelon as if a gift for his mouth. He's in my mirror instantly, of course, and the dust I throw rises like some withering cloud. Mexico, shit, I'm riding inside the belly of the beast, and gone are the McDonald's with hand sanitizers and drive-through coffee.

The sun above, like a record spinning, keeps playing the same old Amboy Dukes' tune, "Journey to the Center of my Mind," and a refrain is stuck in my cochlea like an earworm, "But please realize, you'll probably be surprised, for it's the land unknown to man, where fantasy is fact. Come along if you care, come along if you care, come along to the land inside and you'll see."

Mexico's land unknown to man rolls before me a landscape that rises and falls like its Zen Sea, and the brother outlaws accompanying me — as the Amboy Dukes predicted — confuse fantasy and fact; they weave, wander, and dodge past their imaginary animals. The fat one, on the way to the end of the road, looks like Orson Welles' double leaning over his metal. He burned down his trailer back in Wisconsin for insurance money, and with it bought cocaine and a black poncho. His wife had to crawl through a window to escape because he forgot to tell her. Her hair was singed, her underwear sooty black, but he could have said "slutty black" but never did. He apologized and drove her to the motel where they stayed for the next three weeks B.M. Before Mexico.

The Barbarosa outlaw — close to the front of our pack — we call him Barbarosa for his rusty beard and ponytail and his way of singing old-school country songs, like "Crazy." He's the out-of-control coyote here, like Willie Nelson as the notorious Barbarosa in the 1982 film; and our bad boy has come to a stop. We pull a U-turn and lope toward a cholla cactus. "It needs to be watered," he says, and makes a golden spray. Barbarosa's mouth is full of happy juice and sorrow pebbles he inserts every time he thinks we aren't looking. Mile by mile his hot bone angling for an appointment with pavement and gritty sand, where all the disciples of barley and malt end up sooner than they want. A drunken biker means trouble; the Doobie Brothers sang about this twisted end, "Drink Scotch whiskey all night long and die behind the wheel."

A coyote crosses in the middle of the road, where his chances of survival are not good, and burns a good hard look down the cracked-fingered yellowed pavement. I brake and find myself gazing up into the eyes of a Mexican goddess. She wipes blood and pebbles from my face. I have been laid down like a living zombie on her sofa. I ask her about coyotes, and she laughs.

"Don't move, you sorry gringo," her middle-aged gruff voice tells me. "Let me see where you are damaged the most. My son is looking after your Harley, I think he likes it. He told me it was going to be fine. Penelope is my name, like in Homer — and you have been shipwrecked," she points out.

Blinking sweat from my eyelids, she's not fat but neither is she slim, just old, I observe from my supine position. A fan's whirring in time above my head. No air conditioner. Heat billows from top to bottom, ceiling to floor, squelching flies like a sandwich to the man on a sofa; she wraps my mouth up with a towel full of ice.

I have been cleaned up and I guess my coyote brothers have wandered away without me . . . time warp again . . . when is it? Roadkill, that's what they would say hours later, laughing in their beer and wondering if I'd ever escape Penelope or come back home over the wrecking wall.

Mexico's mangy curs roam the side streets in town, their heads hung low, wary of us and their sharp-toothed coyote cousins that are hanging around just out there, a little way past city limit. Coyotes are smart and hunt in packs, but the curs don't. They're hungry, like the Mexican street vendors, singing their praises for porcelain masks, sugar skulls, and Chicklets.

Driven by empty bellies, curs and vendors move in close, looking past bad experiences with humans, ignoring the warning of our loud machines. The biker who killed the dog said it limped from the side of the road and walked right in front of her. "It committed suicide by motorcycle," she said and wept. "The dog's last look seemed sad, right up to the moment my front tire ran over its skinny body."

We're riding deeper and deeper into a broken territory on a two-wheeled track called *risk*. It's as if reality stalls and the motorcycle dances in time with the dazzling sol of Mexico. With eyes to see, anyone would swear Salvador Dali painted the street where bar balconies, groaning under the weight of heavy bikers, are bowed like snow-covered branches. On the third floor of the Iguana Banana, above the balcony facing the blue sea, a band is kicking out a version of Bowie's "Five Years." Inside the Iguana, I sing along with them, "A cop knelt and kissed the feet of a priest, and a queer threw up at the sight of that."

In tune or out of tune, nobody cared, as the thump-thump of Evolutions announced the schedules be damned 'cause the party's on, and ripe are the two-legged coyotes primed for this biker party happening everywhere. One, in fringed buckskin and patches, says he's from the land of Geronimo. More coyotes arrive to join the sons of Geronimo, and then the risk multipliers show up. They roll in on wavelengths of noise — the Bandidos — adding cock to the cocktail, courting madness and mayhem. They're the mangy cousins of the Apache, and like Geronimo, impossible for the man to catch.

Penelope didn't catch me, but I had a lonely feeling riding toward the wrecking wall that we call a border, and I will miss the fucking Sea of Cortez. Give me shrimp, fiestas, and senoritas, and I could exist forever on sips of Tequila and slices of aguacate. And if Penelope or Mexico's Zen held me long enough, I'd join a mariachi band or go to a Shakespearean play in Spanish. That would be the shit, all those colores brillantes draped on Puck, revving the throttle of "A Midsummer Night's Dream," in a land unknown to man where fantasy is fact.

Border time again, going north, and I'm on the lookout for Carlos Castaneda on his bicycle. Time shifted when he showed up before — or warped — and my Harley took me down and to another place. I'm not nervous going back over the wrecking wall though, because this time I'm going to do what fucking Jack would do and he's got heroic powers. We cross the wall and my brothers go north. I bid adios and go east to New Mexico where tricksters enchant the land, and sunsets slip away, spooky, and lovely.

On the sidewalk in Gallup, a guy stops, leans against the building, and waits with a woman and dog for the walk signal. He's wearing a black jacket and a beret. His jacket is adorned with a large patch on the back and the word *HOCKEY* picturing two stilettoes. Hockey on stilettos, what an idea.

HOCKEY — what an idea, thanks Canada.

TEQUILA — what an idea, thanks Mexico.

A big sign over the Coal Street Pub's door draws me in. I place a toy monster truck in front of me on the bar and give in to desert thirst, ordering a tap beer. I hadn't had one in a while, and when the frosty mug with golden liquid landed next to the monster truck, a husky, loud voice from across the bar offered, "Beer's cold here!" *BANDIDOS* blared across the front of his red, yellow, and black hat. WWFJD?

What do you think about monster trucks? He raised his middle finger.

Got a biker name? "Chopper," he said.

You ride with the Bandidos?

"Yep. That's all I do. I go thousands of miles a month. I love it."

In a driving rainstorm one August night at the Sturgis Motorcycle Rally, far from the Coal Street Pub, thirty Bandidos on choppers rumbled into the campground, dismounted, and slogged through puddles to the social building. The owner tightened up. "They're the worst of the worst," he said. "I've got a shotgun under the bar."

I was wary of the Bandidos in South Dakota and Mexico, but now, sitting across the bar from me in New Mexico, Chopper and I had connected by a mutual hatred for monster trucks and love for motorcycling. I asked if he'd like to hear a story about the monster truck. Poker-faced, in a flat voice, he said, "I like stories."

Four months ago, a few friends and I met along the banks of Lake Superior to commemorate a deceased friend who loathed monster trucks, I said. My friend thought they were perfect symbols of aggression, senseless destruction, and waste. Brilliant, he was, with a dark and complex psychology deep inside. Complex psychologies can define a lot of people: Chopper, Barbarosa and Orson (brothers in my biker pack) and me, I suppose.

Chopper was listening. Our friend loved to travel, I said, and at his memorial, the group thought I should take the monster truck and his spirit riding with it on a motorcycle ride and leave him a place where another traveler could pick it up and keep him moving.

Powered by the energy of squeeze, suck, bang, and blow, I imagined my late friend would be singing a wide-eyed and happy tune, and I believed the chthonic power of bike explosions and the dark revolutions of Dunlop Tires would set his spirit free like a boy galloping on a horse, unhinged, and wild. And then I heard myself ask Chopper to take the truck and my deceased friend for a ride. When you are done, just leave him or pass him on.

Chopper looked and nodded. I knew he understood riding in memory of lost friends. Sending my friend away, galloping from Gallup with the Bandidos on a steel horse of smoke and fire had a ring to it, and it felt strangely divine to me. If the monster truck melted in a fiery pile-up of Harley-Davidsons, at least he'd have one last epic adios — like the way he went out of this world, taking a knife to his own heart.

We talked for a few minutes more, and then Chopper took a phone call. "I got to go meet some brothers," he said, and strutted out the door with an *I am the greatest ever* strut — as Jack would do — and a toy snuggled in his massive, Muhammad Ali-sized hand.

Part of me walked out the door too with Orson, Barbarosa, Chopper, and my friend's spirit in the monster truck. For a moment, back to daydreaming, I disappeared, and a screeching sound . . . a mystical horse with piercing eyes and breath of fire arrived. It drew closer and I heard the drone of dark engine horsepower on Gallup's bad pavement. I imagine a glorious moment of travel. Chopper twisting his wrist and the engine rumbling on to misdeeds unknown, rider's spirits unhinged and cutting razor-sharp lines between life and death while holding the edge on a circle thinner than high desert air.

My daydream was only a moment, then my cloudy eyes sharpened, my daydream cleared, and the loud horse redeposited me back to the Coal Street Pub's barstool and my girlfriend. Under that spell, in a bar on Coal Street, enchantment led me to think of my friend's spirit on a wild ride where Chopper would be his Beatrice, and both would be spinning on the dark circumference of worn treads.

Chopper didn't show it, but awe and fear show up somewhere in every biker's dark night, a soul-place untouched by sonnets for motorcycling, sestinas to Bandidos, iambic pentameters for the Highway to Hell, or haikus to Harley-Davidson. Like Zen, tequila, or coyote, iambic petameter for the Highway to Hell would find a way to reach in and around the dark night and speak to bikers, finding a way past resistance to poems and possibilities in the mysterious.

My wheels are rumbling again, and I have a vision, maybe an enchantment. Jack Nicholson rides in on the Highway to Hell. It's a parade of decibels, diablos, and anxious cops heading to a Bandidos gathering. Jack's going to use his famous voice to speak in iambic petameter where every story gyres deeper in the screw and bikers rev their smutty exhaust. He speaks, bikers listen, and coyotes yip and yelp from the wrecking wall to the mystic blue sea.

Fishing for Her Children / Dave Sims

Rigel 2023 Finalist

SEEING THE SPIDER

LUANN LEWIS

RIGEL 2023 FINALIST

Part I — Diane Saw the Spider

Surely Diane wasn't the only one who saw the spider. It was an ugly little thing . . . white with eight legs, a typical house spider. It was crawling on Allie's back, several inches under her right shoulder. Jeanine's desk was closer to Allie's. Why didn't Jeanine say something? Obviously, Allie didn't *feel* the spider. Her fluffy sweater was too thick.

And the spider wasn't moving particularly fast. Diane might have reached over to brush it off or even whispered something to Allie but the empty desk between Diane and Allie created a chasm that separated them and made it impossible for Diane to let Allie know without yelling or making a scene. Diane didn't want all the kids looking at her. Way back in fourth grade (maybe even earlier), Diane had learned that attention can be a dangerous thing. Attention can mean rubber bands or cruel words shot in your direction. It's better when people don't notice you. So, Diane yawned and gazed up at the ceiling pretending not to see the spider. Still, her eyes were drawn irresistibly back to the spider's journey.

So far the spider had traveled up the lovely curves of Allie's middle back. Yes, Allie had curves, unlike Diane. Even under a fluffy sweater Allie had curves. Allie's hips curved into a trim waist and the boys liked that. Diane imagined how it must feel to be Allie, posing in front of a mirror twisting back and forth. What was it like to walk down the street or through the halls at school or anywhere? Of course, Allie must be full of confidence;

Diane would be too if she had a body like Allie's. How incongruent that a spider would dare crawl on her.

Uh oh, it looked like the spider was heading for Allie's hair, for the long end of the ponytail dangling down. Diane stared, holding her breath. But Allie laughed at something the teacher said then bobbed her head as she turned to exchange glances with Gail who was sitting next to her. This caused the spider to return to its original languid course heading toward Allie's right shoulder. How long would it take the spider to reach Allie's neck? Would it get there before the end of class? There was only ten minutes more to go. Once it got to her neck, would she feel it? Would she turn around and yell at Diane, wondering why Diane didn't say anything? Maybe not.

Maybe the spider was drawn to the delicate sparkling chain clasped above Allie's sweater, resting on the nape of Allie's vulnerable neck. Maybe the spider thought the chain was an inviting web or someplace to nestle.

Allie's silver horse charm would be hanging from that chain. Everybody knew about Allie's horse. It represented the young stallion that Allie's uncle had given her for her sixteenth birthday. Allie had everything. Good looks, good grades, popularity. What else would she get for her sixteenth? How many other girls got a horse for their sixteenth birthday? And Allie had a huge party. Of course Diane hadn't been invited.

Diane had never been a friend of Allie's. Diane lived in Blaston which was west of where Allie lived. The kids from the west were ignored by the kids from the east, who lived in Flagsdale. Now, in high school, the difference in caste was very clear. The low-class west side kids took the bus while the east side kids zipped to school in dazzling new cars, laughing and carefree.

But it wasn't just in high school that one could spot the differences. Way before that, back in grade school, they all sensed the difference. The east side girls with their little Gymboree jumpers and tightly coiffed braids were aware that they were somehow superior to the west side tots with their unruly tangles and baggy hand-me-downs. The east-siders came to school with faces and fingernails scrubbed shiny. The west-siders were sticky with peanut butter and Playdough. Each side played with their own.

So, Diane wondered, why did she even care if a spider was crawling up Allie's back. Diane flipped her pencil back and forth between her fingers. The spider paused. How much harm could it do anyway? Diane's lips suddenly felt rosy, relaxed and smiley. She leaned back in her chair and thrust her legs out. Let's just watch.

Diane glanced to the left and to the right. How come nobody else was saying anything to Allie? Did everybody dislike her as much as Diane did? Was everybody else jealous like she was because, to be honest, Diane had to admit she was more than a bit envious of everything Allie had. Did people really not see this spider or did they simply not want to tell Allie? Which was it?

Or, wait a minute . . . was everybody wondering about Diane? Was everybody wondering why Diane wasn't telling Allie? Were they thinking she was a horrible person for not saying anything? Diane sat up a little. She didn't want people whispering about *her*, gossiping about how awful it was that she had let this spider crawl up Allie's back. What if they were all waiting for her to do something? She glanced left and right again but nobody seemed to be looking at her. Or were they? Was Jeanine giving her the eye? No, Diane guessed not. She bit her lip. Maybe she *should* tell Allie . . . just get up quietly and tap her on the shoulder or just brush the stupid spider off of her. Then Allie would be grateful and thank her, maybe she'd even invite Diane to sit with her at lunch.

Yeah, right. Fat chance. She'd probably just raise her eyebrows and whisper to her friends — "lesbo." Allie might claim there hadn't even been a spider, that Diane just wanted to touch her. Well, forget it. She hoped the spider would bite Allie . . . right in the jugular.

Halting for a moment, the spider rubbed its legs as if it was dancing or spinning a web and Diane shuddered. Ugh, how horrible it would be to have that on your back. She shook her shoulders a bit, just in case somehow there was another spider in the room and it was actually on Diane's own person. Then Allie's spider resumed its slow journey up her sweater. Glancing at the clock, Diane noted that there were only four more minutes left before the bell. She should say something. No she shouldn't. Screw Allie. What did she care? Oh man, it was getting harder to see the spider because it was sort of camouflaged by Allie's thick blonde ponytail whisking back and forth. Diane expected the spider to be caught up in that but somehow it managed to stay the course on Allie's back.

Would Diane be able to live with herself if she didn't let Allie know about that beast crawling towards her neck? Would she forever wonder if there was a spider on her own back that somebody wasn't telling *her* about?

Fighting the urge to bite her nail, she considered the options. Diane fidgeted, foot tapped, leg jiggled, desk squeaked, but she said nothing and the bell rang.

Allie scooped up her books and slid from her seat following her friends out of the classroom, laughing and chatting. Diane dragged her books and papers together and held them to her chest. She made her way through the door and into her future.

Lying in her bed that night she wondered whatever happened with the spider. Did Allie finally feel it and scream, sweep it off her shoulder or neck or did one of her friends see it and rescue her with a squeal and nervous laughter? Diane would never know because she didn't have the nerve (or maybe desire) to tell Allie. Perhaps the spider bit Allie. Maybe two sharp little teeth pierced Allie's white neck, right next to that chain, and tainted Allie's blue blood forever.

From time to time Diane would recall Allie's spider. Occasionally she would remember it regretfully, as something she should have done. A creeping remorse would crawl on Diane's own shoulder, whispering in her ear and telling her she deserved her west side shame. Other times, she imagined the spider riding home in Allie's pony tail and living a long life in Allie's pillow — just to knock the east-sider down a little bit.

Deep in her heart, though, Diane knew that whatever the outcome, the spider on Allie likely only stayed for an afternoon. The spider on Diane would be living there forever.

Part II — Mr. West Saw the Spider

She looked good. He wasn't a pervert or anything, but so many of these girls looked honey-drippin' fine. Going home night after night to Virginia and the kids . . . well, it could be tough for him after being surrounded by all of this blossoming young flesh. He tried not to dwell on their sensuality but when these young women leaned over his desk or passed close to him in the hall, their scent would tweak his instincts. And that Allie Johanson, she made him feel like a jackal sniffing out a passing rabbit. With any of those girls, there were times a soft arm would touch his or a hip would accidentally graze him. How could a normal man not react? After all, Kevin was only thirty-two; there was a lot of life left in his loins. Just 'cuz he was married and had kids didn't mean he was dead. Virginia might not have a lot of energy when it was time to hit the sack, but Kevin always seemed to have enough for "couple time," especially after a day of looking at firm thighs, breasts and shining faces.

Travis, the other male math teacher, from down in the east wing, saw them all as kids. You could tell by his heavy brow and patronizing talk, but Travis turned fifty last year. Kevin wondered if he, himself, would be dead like that at fifty. He doubted it. No matter how much Kevin tried, these girls were never gonna be kids to him, at least not all of them, even if he had to pretend they were. And pretend he did.

But there she was, Allie Johanson, rear swiveling as she moved towards her next class, surrounded by her gaggle of friends, blonde hair bobbing. She had curves no girl her age should have and, oh man, that sweater looked so soft. He wondered how it would feel to rub the cloth between his fingertips, to rest his cheek against it . . . and then he saw the spider.

The ugly little thing simply rode along on Allie's back (Kevin wished HE could ride Allie's back — lucky spider). It sat comfortably, hiding under a bit of sweater fuzz. Kevin could take this opportunity, he thought, to reach out and brush it off, innocently. He imagined the robustness of her shoulder blade, the firm flesh under the sweater. She might turn, eyes wide, surprised to see it was Mr. West. He'd chuckle and let her know that he had saved her from a horrible fate. Would she smile, charmed, happily relieved? He wasn't quite sure. Not known for her sweetness, Allie could easily flout him with some snarky comment. The thought of her friends laughing at him from behind lowered eyelids with twisted, knowing, smiles. "*Sure there was a spider, Mr. West,*" was daunting. He didn't care for scorn and even a hint of improper behavior could be the kiss of death for a teacher. *Better not to touch her.* Yeah, maybe he should just leave the spider on that little bitch. She'd never been a big fan of his anyway, not like the other girls, so why should he bother helping her out now.

He had been friendly enough to her in the past but she acted as if she was a little too smart to be in his class. Sure, she should have been in AP math, they both knew it, but he wasn't going to give her the satisfaction. While the other girls flocked around his desk and laughed at his jokes, Allie hung back and looked at her watch until the bell rang. She had no interest in impressing him and certainly wasn't impressed *by* him. If she had been a bit more agreeable, perhaps he would have considered bumping her up to AP. They could have had that conversation as affable comrades bonding over a conjunct agreement, Allie beaming on him in gratitude. But if she was going to be a snob, forget it. She already had everything handed to her . . . looks, money . . . he even heard from the other kids that her uncle bought her a horse for her sixteenth birthday. A horse! What the heck? Who gets a horse for their birthday?

Yeah, let her walk around with the spider on her stuck-up little back. Somebody would brush it off eventually, one of her many admirers, one of her suck-up little buddies. Kevin had more important things to worry about. He turned down the hall and headed toward his homeroom. Still, he wondered, what would it have been like to touch that sweater. How would that body have felt under his hands? Into what sort of heaven would her perfume send him and how would her breath feel on his lips. He hated wondering these things but he wondered them nevertheless with agonizing waves of pleasure causing him to wonder all the more.

Crawling into bed like a spider, all arms and legs, Kevin swung his body over Virginia and began to kiss her neck. Her jagged breathing plowed into his ear and he pulled away slightly. Closing his eyes, he tried to get the image of Allie Johanson out of his head, but momentarily gave in and allowed himself to be spun into a fantasy of cool blond hair and smooth pink skin. Still, that damn spider kept dangling in the way of all his fun.

Part III — Tim Algrand Saw the Spider

Much earlier that same day, under the bright classroom lights, the spider had appeared white but in reality had been brown. The spider, simply looking for warmth as the season changed, found its way into the ceiling. School had started, the leaves colored and a cool wind was blowing in. All those bodies made the indoor temperature toasty.

There was no particular reason the spider had picked this classroom or this desk but it began to spin a long strand and lowered itself, bit by bit, over Allie's unsuspecting back. Tim Algrand watched the slow movement with fascination. He bit his nails, the long sleeve of his flannel shirt getting in his mouth, as the spider dangled, swinging in a bit of a breeze. Tim hoped the breeze would blow it to the side or maybe that the spider would be startled by something and change its mind and retreat to the ceiling, but it continued to lower itself steadily toward poor Allie Johanson. Its destination was inevitable.

Tim didn't feel good about this but he wasn't sure how he could help. Allie was way out of his league. Already fighting a stutter, his tongue wouldn't know how to warn her. Whatever he might say would come out too loud. It would sound awkward and be completely wrong, so he just wouldn't say anything at all. He could only stare at the course the spider was taking.

Glancing over at Greg Patterson, Tim realized Greg was watching the spider too. Their eyes met. Greg grinned and gave a thumbs up but Tim was feeling worse and worse. The spider hung on its strand, spinning and lowering itself until it rested comfortably on Allie's back, about where her bra would have crossed under her sweater. (Tim's face colored at that thought.)

Yes, Tim would have liked to say something. He felt like maybe he owed Allie. Once, in third grade, Allie made some kids stop picking on him. She had been passing by the arts and crafts table. Paul Overton, Jenna Parsons and Joe Miles were mocking Tim's speech, making up crazy sentences with loud stutters and Allie came by with a frown, condemning them as bullies and telling them they should be ashamed of themselves. Since she was a popular girl even back then, those kids backed off and pretended it was all just a friendly joke.

In spite of her heroics at that time, Allie wasn't known for her kindness. Her rep was as a sarcastic foe; her humor could bite. Some kids disliked her because of it, but Tim continued to remember when he was eight years old and the time she rescued him. Now he felt distinctly uncomfortable allowing the spider to settle onto her sweater. Still, somehow he couldn't muster up the courage to do something as simple as move over and knock the damn thing off. Greg, on the other hand, appeared to be enjoying the spider's journey. He had leaned back in his chair, one arm crossed over his chest, and was tapping the top of a pen against his chin. Malicious smile on his face, he made crawling motions with his fingers when Tim looked his way.

Tim, however, was consoling himself by believing that one of Allie's friends would see the spider and take care of the problem. Certainly, he assured himself, that's how it would work out. After all, she had dozens of friends. They would come to her rescue, wouldn't they? Hell, she probably wouldn't even want a dweeb like him to take care of her.

And the spider just sat there; at least it wasn't moving. Tim supposed that if it had been crawling around, he would have had to do something about it. He would have had the courage then, wouldn't he? But it wasn't moving now, right? It wasn't doing any harm. Why get all upset about nothing? Allie probably didn't even remember him from third grade anyway. She wasn't expecting a payback.

Greg raised his eyebrows and smirked at Tim who smiled back, lips stiff and throat tight. I'm not a mean guy, he thought to himself, I don't really think it's funny that the spider's there. But he high-fived Greg when class ended and they snickered together as they watched Allie leave the classroom. Hell, it's just a spider. So what?

Part IV – Allie Saw the Spider

I had a fucking spider in my hair. A fucking spider. I hate spiders. I was lying on my bed, reading, and all of the sudden it was on my forehead. I know it came out of my hair because, at first, I thought it was just a strand from my ponytail but then I realized it was a spider! I sat up and screamed. Of course, I immediately pounded the damn thing to death with my book but I don't know how long it was there. I couldn't stop shaking. So disgusting.

But that's how it is with me. It's like I'm marked. I'm a magnet for bugs and disgusting things. When I was thirteen I went to summer camp in Wisconsin. I was the only girl that got a frog in her bed. Nobody put it there, it just found me. It's like there's something wrong with me. I'm tainted. Bugs crawl on me, frogs get in my bed. Really, I'm totally tainted.

You know, I try to laugh it off and pretend it's nothing, but stuff like this happens to me all the time. Bees chase me and they never seem to chase after anybody else. Ants crawl toward my picnic food but leave everyone else's alone. It's always like this for me. Other people don't notice, but I do. I always notice. There's something about me. And whatever it is has always been there.

Wherever I'm at, I attract the repulsive. When I was little, there was this guy at the bus stop, he was wearing a nice business suit and carrying an expensive looking briefcase. There were other people around, but guess who's leg he touched? Yep, mine. He put his hand on my leg and moved it up my thigh and I was only about nine. Of course I shouldn't have even been at the bus stop by myself but my parents were too busy to take me to dance class so they sent me on my own.

And a couple of years later, there was this guy outside the 7-11 who pushed me against the dumpster and well, ground himself into me. All I wanted was a stupid peanut butter cup but I couldn't even get into the store. This guy pulled me to the back. I had to kick him in the crotch and run away, heart pounding, breath barely making it out of my lungs. And even before all that stuff, my uncle — well, he's not really my uncle, he's just a friend of my mom's — he made me take off my shirt and my panties and then started kissing me. He told me he had to do that because of the way I looked at him. There was something about me, he said. And he's right. There *is* just something about me.

I don't like to go to the beach because things touch me in the water. Maybe it's fish, maybe not. Maybe it's disgusting things . . . dark swimming things that I don't know the names for. I'd much rather swim in a pool where I can see what's coming at me, where I can see what's going on. Actually, I'd just rather not swim at all. My uncle used to give me swimming lessons in the summer and let me tell you, I was happy each year when autumn would roll in. During the warm weather my uncle and his friends hung around a lot. Mom was happy to have them there, serving them lemonade, making them food. They'd laugh and make jokes with her but then yell for me to come out and swim with them. At least in the fall, when we'd run in the leaves, I'd be able to wear my jeans and a jacket, not just a skimpy bathing suit. But my mom is crazy about my uncle. She's crazy about all of my uncles.

Everybody talks about how my Uncle Randolph bought me the horse. And, man, I love that horse. I would do anything for that horse. He gave me a little silver necklace to mark the day, he said, and told me he was glad that I don't make fusses or tell secrets. He said I was a good girl but we both know I'm not. We both know that there's something wrong with me. I'm quiet about it. I'm quiet about the uncles, but I'm definitely not good. Look at me. Look at that dead spider. I'm telling you, I attract ugly things.

Hope Your Heart Is Lighter Than a Feather / Quentin Pace

Rigel 2023 Best of Art

A Brief History of a Flood

J Carraher

Rigel 2023 Best of Essay

It's been raining here for what seems like months. We've spent seven years praying for water and three whistling *The Fire Next Time.* The laguna has flooded across roads and winter crops; grapevine trellises poke out like dock pilings from the brown and murky water brought up by a decade of hard cracked earth and fires that just two summers ago tore through our backyards and turned the sky a dark ginger all the way across the Golden Gate, blotting out the September sun, moving daytime to dusk.

The orchard where we live is plentiful with apples, summer into autumn. It sits atop a small hill so that we can hear the Atascadero creek running below us; today it sounds almost like the sea, having eaten its own banks and carved a new path through the pasture where sheep and donkeys stand knee-deep in its flows. It doesn't reach our cellar or lap the sunroom floor, already dampened from the windblown rain, for the small rise of this place. The baler across the road is submerged nearly to its roof. You can just see the uppermost treads of the combine harvester that was worked nearby in summer but has disappeared in the dark waters, rising inch by inch, day by sodden day.

My little son says he's a mycologist and the floods seem to make him so. He eyes the red dappled caps of the fly agaric which grow as big as dinner plates under the redwoods lining the neighbor's backyard vineyard. He says the ground cover is spotted collybin. He knows this because it looks like challah that has been in the oven too long, he says. He explains waxy caps and every detail of the sulfur tuft, the redwood rooter, digs deep into the dirt until his fingers turn pink from the cold and his soft, still-baby skin folds in on itself from the damp, bringing up truffles, cupped in his long-fingered hand. He tells me, if you are a *real* mycologist, such as he, you can tell them apart by smelling the gills or spores, or even, when you find the little brown mushrooms, so hard to identify by sight and smell, you can taste them, but only if you are an expert.

I am reminded of my life in the Pacific Northwest where, as a child, I would break apart fungi that I found on fallen trees in the woods behind my grandparents' red brick house, the one I still dream of walking through some nights. I tell my little son how I would peel it just so and tuck it into the front pocket of my coveralls so that later I could reach to stroke its velvety innards when I was scared or alone in the woods. *Mama*, he says, *that was a foliose; it's lichen, not a mushroom.* And I am happy. I exalt this child who already has such a deep love for a small detail of his expanding universe, such enchantment, that he has taught himself more about this one single thing than I will ever know, perhaps about anything.

He is eight years old.

I get a familiar jolt when the pager alerts from my pocket telling me to phone a patrol officer or detective who has responded to an assault in our county. It is my job to call back, establish a timeframe, *acute or historical.* I am to take down the details of the assault: *what part of whose body went where, was the victim conscious or unconscious, are we talking about an adult or a child* and arrange to meet the detectives at the local hospital or children's center for a forensic interview and exam. On this day I call the detective, the one with the ultra-clean, snakeskin cowboy boots, the one who is too tall to talk to, really, and maybe that's why I can never remember his name. Too Tall gives me the details of a child who has been raped by her very own father in her very own home, in the living room while they were watching television. I wonder what she was watching and if she can ever see it again without the dark memory of being in danger in her very own living room with her very own father. I learn that they were discovered by her mother who had gone out to the market or to pick up a brother from basketball practice or for a drink with friends, because you can do that when your daughter is safe in her very own home with her very own father.

The distraught and raging mother has driven her child, her only daughter, two loose plaits hanging over either shoulder and wrapped in a favorite blanket with bunnies on, to the community hospital, for that is where we go for help, even if there is no help there. There is no help because doctors are busy trying in vain to fix someone's grandfather who is in cardiac arrest or stroking out, the woman pregnant with twins who is suffering a brain aneurysm. They're trying to fix the kid who accidentally put an ax into his femoral artery while chopping wood for the stove and is bleeding out all over his gurney and onto the waxy floor. They are busy restraining the man, who is barely a man, only eighteen years old, on a psychiatric hold for delusions of walking through his dead grandparents' house at night. There is no help here.

Nurses are tired and cranky, having not eaten or peed in more than eleven hours and *don't really have time*, they say to the charge nurse, for a hysterical mother and her healthy seeming little daughter. But one young nurse who started working here just last week, sees the fear in the girl's face and hears the pleas in the mother's rising, trilling voice. This Young Nurse asks the right questions and, still new enough to be horrified, still open enough to be determined, still recalling from her training what mandated reporting means, picks up the receiver to report the details to the Too Tall Detective, details that she too, will take home with her tonight.

I try to make it to yoga class every morning these later-life days. I am told that the most important part of yoga is to find a daily foundation. *What is your intention today? Set an intention for your practice.* Every morning we sit in Sukhasana, hands resting on the knees, palms raised toward the sky, open to the universe. We are told to think about the way the body moves, about what accomplishments this vessel might make in a practice, in a day, in a lifetime. We are asked to *close down* our eyes and set the intention. *Write a word behind your eyes. See that word throughout your practice.*

What's the next step? asks Too Tall after he painstakingly delivers all of the details to me. I have listened while I watch my son, fingers deep in the earth, sniffing caps and stems pinched between knowing fingers. But I wait. Next steps. *Breathe in. Set an intention. Watch the breath descend down your spine; imagine its color.* I imagine it blue. *Exhale. When you think you have extinguished all breath, release a little more. Let it go from the base of your spine, through your heartspace, Anahata. Let it flow, like water . . .* like the water that flows by the feet of my son as he uncovers the earth. I look at him, this impossibly small vessel and then it surfaces, the blue of the water behind my eyes.

The victim, the detective tells me, is eight years old.

I think of pranayama when the Too Tall Detective tells me the details of this child's assault. *Breathe all the way out, from the base of your spine through your heartspace. Invite your soul to live there.* I imagine prana, her lifeforce, the lifeforce of other victims. Young women or old, young men or not, whose bodies, I am sure they too imagined as vessels, saw the universe opening, full of possibilities at the beginning of this, the worst day. *Let's begin with the yogic mantra that allows us to contemplate the mystery of being:* So-*hum*. I chant. *I am that.*

We go inside, my little son and I. I run a bath. I put him in and watch the water run brown from his fingers, off his elbows and belly, from his kneeling and his digging, run brown like the Atascadero outside our back door. I change my clothes and make tea with honey. I tell my husband goodbye, I will see you when the sun comes up, or has shone through the rain, and walk into the blue. I pull the car slowly across the long, gravel drive toward the barlow and make my way away from them, into the deep of it.

I think of our eight-year-old as I drive to her. At the beginning of this day, what was her intention? What word did the boy who I saw last week write behind his eyes and does it remain etched there when his wrists and ankles are bound? Or when the legs of the woman I saw on Friday are stretched into *upavistha konasana*, does her single word *light, hope, service, joy*, the name of a lover or a child from here forward carry the weight of this, her darkest fate? *Imagine it. Write it behind your eyes. Purnasya purnamadaya. Remove this whole from that whole; what remains is still whole.* How can that be?

At the end of practice we lie supine, the final resting pose savanasa, legs out, arms at the sides of the body, eyes closed, *soften the breath*. The pose is said to embody total relaxation and is thus the hardest. It is also the corpse pose, the pose of death. I wonder how many times before she was eight years old she changed into her sleeping clothes, climbed beneath her blanket for the night, *ujjayi breath*, prostrate, corpse pose, laying in wait, soft breath, no breath, he's out there, just beyond the door, *close your eyes down, bhramari pranayama*, humming bee breath, *calm the mind*, if you don't move he won't see you, corpse pose, *write your intention behind your eyes, dear one. Don't touch me. Don't touch. Don't.*

I arrive at the hospital, half soaked through from the walk from the lot to the exam room and with a heaviness I feel but cannot see. I lifted my son from the bath before leaving home, dried him with a warm, soft bath towel, dressed him for bed in his favorite red plaid pajamas. All the while I thought through my questions for the victim's mother: *Your child, has she eaten or had anything to drink? Have you changed her clothes? Has she been bathed*? The questions always feel like judgments, like interrogation. *Why haven't you bathed your child?* When what I really mean is: *It is best that you haven't bathed your child so that I can collect the DNA of your husband from her body.*

When you breathe in, imagine no time because time is not, there is only Now which is a precious gift. But time, it is an illusion. For whom, I wonder, for whom? I walk from the car to the backdoor of the hospital, to the after-hours staff entrance which is an ambulance bay for medical emergencies, which this is and is not. As the door closes behind me and I shake the rain from the hood of my coat, water falls on my hair and a single warm drop slides down my cheek like a tear.

I unlock the door to the exam room 1-7-4-2 like a mantra, every door a secret code. Flip on a dim light. Wipe everything down with bleach: countertops, exam table, instruments, toilet, sinks, taps, walls, floor. Evidence collection requires sterile spaces. DNA collection from a body is ensured only by precision. *Write it behind your eyes.* The smell burns my throat and my eyes, which often tear, dripping off my nose onto the counter so that I have to start the sterilization process all over again. *Root yourself to the earth.* Wipe, open lockbox 4-7-3-5, retrieve keys, unlock drawers, files, unlock doors, refrigerator, evidence locker. *When you stand in mountain pose, tadasana, stand firm and erect, as unshakable as a mountain.* Open evidence box, snap the red tape encasement, remove swabs, smaller boxes, envelopes, larger envelopes, biohazard stickers, evidence labels, slides. *Turn your hands toward the thighs and feel the energy. The root of our being is in sacral chakra, the seat of our lifeforce, where all life begins and flows forth, like water.* Remove needles, sterile water, more swabs, more small boxes, bandages, medications, lubricating gel, urine collection cups, alcohol swabs, betadine, a comb for hair collection, pubic hair collection kit, nail brush, bindle for nail clippings, medications, tissue, bandages, more swabs, more swabs, more, boxes and boxes and boxes. *Set your intention and just breathe.*

We are told to let prana flow. Imagine a ball of light circling the chakras to regain and maintain balance between our physical and spiritual bodies. Today we focus on Svadhisthana. *Imagine it as an orange light. Pranayama. Ujiayi breath, through the pubic bone. Imagine a tube and the ball of light passing through each chakra focusing on Svadhisthana, the source of creativity and pleasure.* I am imagining this orange light glowing hot and then darkening, blocked. Svadhisthana represents the relationship between the tides, earth's water, and the phases of the moon. I think of how the moon provides guidance on the darkest of nights and wish for a single beam to guide us through this, for the tide to pull us away. But when I meet my eight-year-old victim and her mother, I lead them from the emergency department to the windowless exam room under watchful eyes of the Young Nurse and accompanied by the Too Tall Detective who will interview the mother while I perform my exam, I hear our eight-year-old whisper, *It's so dark in here, I feel like I can't see.*

Now we will focus on the sacral chakra, we will mark the phases of the moon upon her small body. *Set your intention. Write it behind your eyes.*

There is a flood behind my eyes. I, too, cannot see.

When the rain falls on the roof of the yoga room, which sits inside of a large metal warehouse the contact sounds like little pebbles tossed by birds crossing the sky and creates a rhythm by which I can measure my breath. *Close your eyes down. Write your intention behind your eyes.* The Yogi likes to read from Kahlil Gibran or offer Eckhart Tolle quotes. *As soon as you honor the present moment, all unhappiness and struggle dissolve,* which breaks my intention and leaves me asking how we can live in a world where we don't honor the struggle. *Ujjayi breath. Set a new intention.* I hear the rain fall hard against the studio roof and the wind blow branches off the trees. The windows flash blue from lightning. I wonder, are we to see the rain as cleansing and the intention as *truth* when the waters are so deep that there is no sign of the shore, let alone the ability to reach it? Water, light, grief. I wonder, can a person drown from sadness? *See all of your thoughts, acknowledge them, let them go. Watch them float away.* Behind my eyes I etch *flood.*

When I take the little one by the hand and lead her to the sterile room that is cold and smells of bleach and has no windows, no sounds like birds dropping pebbles nor a rhythm like wind to measure her breath, I tell her, *It's okay. I am here to help you.* I explain how swabs will touch her in places that shouldn't be touched until she is older and never without invitation. I explain to her, this eight-year-old child, how the Too Tall Detective and I will work together, along with all of the people who love her, to keep her safe. I tell her that to do so I will look at her body, all of her body, *Sahaswara to Muladhara*, to touch it with instruments and swabs. I tell her that to *help her* I will have to photograph it, even if I don't believe it. I assure her that she is normal, that she is not damaged. I tell her that she is like any other eight-year-old. *Remove this whole from that whole; what remains is still whole.*

Okay she says, agreeing to all of our invasions (upon invasion) of this impossibly small body, her only vessel. I tell her we, she and I together, will take everything carefully and I will only touch her with her permission every time I touch her. We sit in chairs facing one another, knee to knee, *Sukhasana,* palms raised to the sky. I say, *let's breathe together. Close down your eyes, imagine water, a river flowing out to sea.* She relaxes, breathes deep, for minutes that seem like years. After this long illusion of time, she opens her eyes and looks directly into mine. *I love my dad,* she says. *Don't let them take my dad away.* Write it behind your eyes.

***N**o more water, no more water, no more water but fire next time.*

Salvatore Milione

Maureen D. Hall

Rigel 2023 Best of Fiction

It was a joke, drinking coffee through a straw, like a two-year-old with a sippy cup. *Un insulto.* The way Salvatore's grandson drank juice when he was a small boy. But his grandson had been old enough to drink coffee for years now, though not yet so old as to require a straw doing so. Paul was a father himself, but Salvatore had yet to meet his great-grandchildren. He'd been at Paul's wedding two, maybe three years ago. It was the last time he and Lucia attended a family event outside of this place.

This place. He wouldn't call it what it was: a nursing home. That he and Lucia should end up in a place like this was the biggest failure of his life. Were his parents or grandparents put in a home, God rest their souls, in Italy? No, they were cared for by family, the way God and nature intended. Not by Sal or Lucia, however; they'd left Italy long ago, before the war, after the birth of their first child, Angelo, never seeing their parents or grandparents, their village, again. Maybe that was the first failure. The one that begot all the others. *Il più grande fallimento.*

"You done with your lunch, Sal? Should I leave your coffee?" It was the large black woman whose name he could never remember. He didn't like that she called him Sal, but she was strong, capable. She took good care of Lucia.

"You may take it all." He released his crumpled napkin onto the tray. "The coffee was cold."

"I can heat it up for you."

"Tell me your name again, please?"

"Zuri. It's okay." She leaned over and wiped his face with the crumpled napkin. "It's a hard one for lots of folks here."

"Zu-ree." Salvatore pushed her hand away. "Thank you. I do not need the coffee to be heated."

"Okay then. We'll be back soon to get you to the bathroom, maybe have a little walk."

A little walk. As if he were a dog.

Zuri stopped for Lucia's tray. "You done, Mrs. Mili?"

Salvatore could never decide if it was more respectful or less, the way she called him Sal, but his wife Mrs. Mili. Was it because Lucia spoke only Italian? Their actual surname was Milione. For months after they'd moved to this place, Salvatore had corrected every person who mispronounced it. Even when he gave up, Angelo remained furious, taking it as an insult to their heritage.

But Salvatore observed the nurses and aids who moved Lucia between the bed and the chair, who so efficiently showered and cleaned her, changed her when she was soiled. Things he'd struggled with, mostly on his own, for years. "We let it be," he directed Angelo. "It does not matter."

Lucia was often difficult. And he needed these women to like her, not to feel bad over something as insignificant as a name. Most people here simply called him Salvatore. Either way, he knew who he was. That was all that mattered.

"Lucia is finished," Salvatore told Zuri.

Zuri tried to wipe Lucia's face, but Lucia batted her hand. "Smettila damazione," she instructed. *Stop it, goddamn it.*

"You're welcome." Zuri disappeared with the tray. Salvatore heard the squeaking of the cart progressing down the hall, Zuri's voice in the next room, unfailingly cheerful. She was exhausting.

His wife raised her arm to the doorway, still chastising Zuri, words tumbling out so rapidly even Salvatore couldn't keep up. "Abbastanza," he said. Lucia thrust her arm at him in one swift motion and fell silent.

Their chairs sat on opposite sides of the room, Lucia's by the door, Salvatore's next to the window. Their room was on the third floor. From his chair, all Salvatore could see were tree branches and the other wing of the home, facing the road. He wasn't sure what month it was, but there were buds on the trees. March then, maybe April? Lucia's birthday was in April.

She would be ninety. They should have a party. He would tell Angelo the next time he called.

He needed to pee. "Where is that woman?" he asked Lucia in Italian. This happened all the time. They said they were coming back but they didn't. Too busy or they forgot. Lucia ignored him, intent on the television hanging from the wall, that game show she liked, the one with the models and the doors. He didn't understand her fascination. It wasn't like she could understand most of what they said.

Neither of them spoke English when they came to New York in 1935, September seventh. But Salvatore had learned. It hadn't been easy, working every day in the shop with his cousin, repairing shoes, like his father and grandfather before him in Italy. His cousin, born in New York, spoke English and Italian, and he encouraged Salvatore's English, a good man who died too young, leaving Salvatore to run the shop on his own.

They'd lived in the apartment above. Lucia took care of everything, the cooking, the cleaning, the washing, the accounting for the shop. But she'd refused to learn English. Over the years she absorbed words and phrases, understanding more than she let on. Still, she shopped at the Italian grocers, the Italian butcher. She sought out Father Dominic to hear her weekly confession. Most of their friends spoke Italian.

Salvatore spoke English to their sons to balance the fact that Lucia would not. When Angelo started school, Salvatore was the one who met with his teachers. Lucia stayed home, baking, mending, tending to the babies. She was a good mother. Even so, there were losses, children that died.

Between Angelo and Joseph there was Matteo and Enzo, twins, like Lucia's mother. Enzo died only days old, but Matteo hung on for months, Lucia holding him to her breast, applying poultices to his tiny chest as it fluttered up and down in his struggle for air. The night Matteo passed, Lucia held him for hours, not seeing Salvatore, not hearing his pleas to put the baby down and pick up their living child, Angelo crying on the floor. Father Dominic, accompanied by the ladies from Saint Anthony's, had to come and physically take the dead baby away.

Salvatore's heart broke for her, but hadn't Enzo and Matteo been his sons too? Did she think he was impenetrable, like steel, that he didn't grieve? Or was his heart was made of dirt — mud — disappearing, swallowed down the drain with everyone else's despair, nothing left for him. For weeks he took Angelo every morning to the shop. His cousin's widow cared for the boy afternoons, looking in on Lucia. Till one morning Lucia stopped him as he left the apartment, extending her arms. For a moment, Salvatore had been sure she was going to embrace him, hold him while he cried. Tears filled his eyes.

But no. "Give me," she said in English. And he handed Angelo over.

That night she moved from the couch to Angelo's small trundle bed in the hallway, and Salvatore feared his life was over. What was life without Lucia's smile blossoming on her face as he climbed the stairs each day to find her in the kitchen, humming as she cooked, Angelo standing on a chair, dropping ingredients into the big pot under her watchful eye?

In time she ventured out again, pushing Angelo in the carriage to mass, to the grocer's, the park, but her nights were spent wrapped around their son, and Salvatore slept alone. For months. Finally, he confessed to Father Dominic. "I miss my wife."

"You must be patient," Father Dominic scolded. "Try to control your lust."

Lust? Salvatore rose from kneeling in the tiny confessional and walked out, his breath strangled by anger. The priest might be a man of God, but he did not have a wife. He hadn't been in love with Lucia since she was thirteen. He didn't remember her clutching a straggly bunch of flowers on their wedding day, her bright eyes peeking out at him mischievously from under her veil. The priest had never lay in her arms, retching, on the crowded ship when they came to America, just the three of them, Angelo an infant, Lucia barely twenty.

Salvatore fled in the rain to his shop, pounding nails through leather, destroying boots he would stay up all night repairing while he wept. In the morning, Lucia brought him bread and sausage, and without looking up, he motioned for her to leave it on the counter. They did not speak.

He worked long into that next night, the apartment dark, silent, when finally he climbed the stairs. Lucia and Angelo did not stir in their bed when Salvatore rested his callused palm across his son's dark curls before washing, stripping to his underwear, and climbing into his own empty bed.

The sun had just cast a beam of light through the bedroom curtain when Salvatore felt Lucia climb into their bed. She was tiny and the mattress barely moved. Salvatore lay facing the wall, frozen, his heart beating wildly, hands clenched in fists beneath his cheek. Minutes went by before Lucia tugged at his shoulder, pulling him onto his back. She rested her head on his chest, arm across his belly, his hand grazing her hip. They lay like that, motionless, till Angelo woke up, padding across the chilly floor, crawling in beside them.

Had Father Dominic sought her out? Or had Salvatore's silence pierced her heart? He never asked and Lucia didn't explain. A year later, sweet Joseph was born. They'd never slept apart again. Not until they were forced into this place.

"Where she go?" Salvatore pulled off his glasses, pressing the call light, tied to the wooden arm of his chair. "Why she not come?" He leaned forward, head bent over his knees, pushing himself to stand. "Merda."

"Madonna santa," Lucia exclaimed. "No, Salvatore!"

"Tutto bene, Lulu." Salvatore steadied himself, one hand on the heating duct under the window, the other caressing the air in Lucia's direction. "Tutto bene."

He took two tentative steps. There was no carpet and the floor was slippery beneath his socks. But his slippers were lost, kicked under the bed. If he made it to the wall he'd hold the bathroom door, and then the sink and the bars by the toilet.

He wasn't supposed to get up or walk without help. When they'd moved here, he pushed Lucia in her chair, walked alone every day: the bathroom, the nurses station, the outdoor terrace on the second floor, even the lobby, where the receptionist watched him with an eagle eye. As though he might take off and abandon Lucia in that hellhole.

Then he fell. And fell again, several times these last months, leading to new orders, confining him to his chair, short walks in the hallway with supervision.

He rested against the bathroom door before slowly inching one foot onto the tile.

"Sal!" The large woman imploded into the room. "What are you doing?"

Startled, Salvatore pitched forward, grasping the sink. One hand slipped, his head banging hard against the porcelain rim. Zuri — *that was her name!* — gripped him under both arms, setting him upright.

"Are you okay?"

"I need to pass the water." Salvatore's voice shook, his head pounding where it hit the sink. He felt the release of his bladder, urine trickling down his leg, drenching his trousers. "Too late." He shook his head.

Zuri sighed, pulling on latex gloves from the box behind the sink. "Let's get you cleaned up." She tugged his trousers and underwear down before easing him onto the toilet.

"You didn't come back," Salvatore said softly.

"I know." She gathered his wet things off the floor. "I'm sorry."

The phone rang and Salvatore's eyes flew open. It was out of reach, on the nightstand behind him. The woman, whose name he never remembered, had tied him to the chair.

"I have no choice, Sal," she'd insisted. "You could fall and break a hip." Across the room Lucia had sobbed silently, hands hiding her face.

"Please." He was humiliated. "Don't use the rope." He knew it was a Posey, a vest restraint and not a rope. *Posey, ha! Like a flower and not a noose.* But when it slipped over his head, trapping him in the chair, he felt like a calf, a pig, tied up for slaughter.

"I'll be back to loosen it."

But she didn't come back. And Salvatore had fallen asleep, chin resting against his chest, drool inching down the bib of the restraint.

The phone kept ringing. He reached for the call light, pumping the button with his thumb. "Please, someone help me! The phone, please." Lucia stirred in her chair but did not wake up.

A woman ran in, a girl really, with a long ponytail, her white uniform bulging in a circle around her waist. She lifted the phone receiver and handed it to Salvatore, moving the whole contraption to the tray table in front of him. "I'll be back," she whispered.

He barely heard her. "Hello?" he sputtered into the phone. "Who this is?"

"Pop, it's Joseph."

Ah, Joseph, the sweetest boy on the earth, even at seventy. Or was it Angelo who was seventy? "Joseph, *mimmo*. You call your papa, such a good boy. And Marie? How she is?"

"You mean Kathryn." Joseph paused. "Marie is Angelo's wife, Pop. Or she was. Kathryn's fine. We're all fine."

"Kathryn, yes, I am so sorry." Salvatore switched the phone to his good ear. He glanced over at Lucia to see if she'd heard him mention Marie. But she slept on, thank God.

Marie and Angelo divorced years ago; Salvatore knew that. It was scandalous, a family crisis. Lucia didn't speak to Angelo for months. Salvatore was more philosophical. Life was short, his son deserved happiness in his marriage. Marie's grandparents were from Sicily, which technically made her Italian. She was cold and rarely laughed. He and Lucia never much cared for her. After the divorce they seldom saw their two grandsons, very sad. Joseph and Kathryn had only daughters, three of them. Kathryn's people were Finnish, but she'd converted to Catholicism when they married, which had thrilled Lucia and endeared Kathryn to them both.

"Joseph, when I see you? It's been a very long time."

"Pop, we were there last weekend. Remember, we had brandy and Kathryn made cannolis?"

"Yes, I remember, but seems so long." Brandy? Lucia was the one who liked brandy, the one who taught Kathryn how to make cannoli. Salvatore looked out the window, the bare branches swaying in the breeze, the sun low in the late day sky. Where had the day gone? "Joseph, she use the rope again. You tell them not to do this, no?"

"I know, Pop, that's why I called. They said you almost fell, that you hit your head."

"It's nothing. Niente." Salvatore rubbed the bump over his right eye. "Tell them I cannot have the rope. Is too tight. I cannot breathe."

"You can't get up by yourself," Joseph said. "It's the only way to stop the rope."

"I'm sorry. I had to pass the water."

Joseph paused. "I'm the one who's sorry, Pop. It's hard, I know."

"We make a birthday party for your mama." Salvatore changed the subject. "She will be ninety on April the 18th."

"She'll be ninety-two," Joseph corrected. "We had a party when she turned ninety. Remember, they let us use the private dining room? All the grandkids came."

"Well, we have the party for ninety-two then. Is important, no?"

"Very important," Joseph agreed. "I'll talk to Kathryn. We'll figure something out."

"If Mama is ninety-two, I am ninety-eight?" Salvatore asked. "Cannot be possible."

"Tell me about it. I'll be seventy soon, an old man." Joseph laughed. "Wait till you're a hundred, Pop. That'll be the biggest party ever."

"I be dead long before that. My Nonina, she live to one hundred and two. She still make the bread and feed the chickens, they say." Salvatore shook his head at the phone, like Joseph was in the room and could see him. "But me? I am in the chair with the rope." The aide with the ponytail hovered in the doorway. "I go now, Joseph. The girl is here."

"Give Mom a kiss for me. And Pop? I love you."

"I know you do." Salvatore hung up the phone. "You are a good boy."

"Hola, Mr. Mili." The girl walked past his sleeping wife, past the TV, over to his chair. "Buenos días."

"You are the Spanish girl. Buongiorno." Salvatore's face lit up. "Remind me your name." He liked this one. She called him Mr. Mili and she spoke a little Spanish to him, which wasn't too far from Italian, a game they shared. Sometimes she understood a few words of Lucia's gobbledygook.

"Anna. I'm Puerto Rican, but whatever." She shrugged. "You get the idea."

"Anna, my daughter's name." He lowered his voice, peeking sideways at Lucia. How could he ever forget the name Anna? "She die, only five years old. What they call? The blood cancer."

"I know. It's really sad." Anna ran her finger gently over the bump on his brow. "I'm sorry you needed the rope. How's about I untie you and we go for a walk?"

"A walk, yes." This one, Anna — like his daughter — always took him out of the room. She came when she said she would. A treasure.

The girl's pocket buzzed, and she pulled one of those little radio-like phones from it, the kind his children and grandchildren carried everywhere. "Hold on, Mr. Mili. I gotta take this." She went into the bathroom, closing the door. Still, Salvatore heard the rise and fall of her voice. There was yelling. When she came out her eyes were red.

"You cry," Salvatore said.

"My boyfriend's a jerk sometimes." She took a big breath. "I'm okay. Let's get you to the bathroom."

She untied the restraint and helped him to his feet.

"I do myself," he reminded her.

"I'm just along for the ride."

Salvatore made his way to the toilet, Anna hovering close behind. He grasped the bars on either side of the commode, and she unzipped his trousers, holding on while he lowered himself to the seat. "I have to move the bowels." He waved her away. "Close the door. I call you."

She didn't seem surprised. "Don't get up without me." She stood outside the partially closed door. "I'm right here."

He'd grown used to relieving himself in the presence of strangers, but that never made it any less mortifying. When he finished, he tore a few squares of toilet paper from the roll and tried to wipe. "Can you come?" he called. "Is too hard."

"I got you." Anna came in, gloves on. She cleaned him, supporting him while they washed their hands. "Okay," she said, "now we walk."

"I am too tired," Salvatore complained.

"Tough." Anna took his arm and led him to the hallway. "Should we wake your wife up? She freaks out when you're gone."

It was true. Last year they took him in an ambulance to the hospital with chest pain, keeping him overnight. Lucia cried and screamed until finally they had to sedate her.

"We let her sleep." Salvatore stopped and rested his hand on her hair. It was gray with white streaks, short now, washed and set in the first-floor beauty parlor every other week. She always came back smiling.

He held onto the rail. It was a long way to the nurses' station. "You go ahead," Salvatore told her. But Anna stuck to his side, occasionally touching his elbow. "You are in school?"

"Senior year. You remembered." She grinned. "My mom wants me to go to college and be a nurse. But I don't know. It's a lotta science."

"You are smart. You study, work hard." Salvatore stopped walking, pointing his finger at her. "You do this, no?"

"Okay, okay."

She settled him in a chair across from the nurses' station, bringing him a cup of chocolate milkshake and a small bag of Chips Ahoy. "I know you like Lorna Doones, but they didn't send any up today."

"Grazie." He pulled on the straw. "Is good."

"I'll be back in a bit. Don't move."

Salvatore looked around the nurses' station, chewing his cookies, sipping the shake. Sitting nearby, the same four or five women as always, two in wheelchairs. One was missing a leg, her other foot, swollen, red, propped up with pillows. Diabetes.

"Hello, Salvatore," she said.

"Buongiorno."

"Tessie Epstein. We've met." She held her heavily bejeweled hand to her bosom, bracelets clacking.

He nodded. "I remember." She was insufferable, constantly ordering the nurses around as though they were her servants.

"Look at my shoe, Salvatore." A short nurse with large hoop earrings and braids held her foot out, the toe of her shoe flopping open.

"If I had my tools, I fix for you," he said. "I used to repair the shoes."

"That's why I showed you, hon." She leaned over and ruffled his hair. "Everything is crap these days. I bet none of your shoes fell apart."

He patted his hair back into place. "My shoes the best."

"What happened to your head?" Mrs. Hurley pointed her cane. "That's quite a bruise."

"It's not that bad," the nurse with the earrings said.

"Get the man some ice," Tessie directed.

A white nurse Salvatore didn't recognize brought him a latex glove dripping with ice. "Let me hold that on your head, doll."

"*I* do." He took the glove, resting it over his eyebrow till she walked away. Then he covertly dropped it to the floor, kicking it under his chair.

"Oh, my." Mrs. Hurley giggled. "I saw nothing." She rose, leaning on her cane, slowly making her way down the opposite wing.

"How you doing, Mr. Mili?" Anna, back, just as she'd promised. "You ready to roll?"

"I am ready." He stood up, bowing his head at the remaining women.

They heard Lucia long before reaching the room. "Can someone shut her up?" An old lady leaning on a walker snapped at them as they shuffled by.

"She'll quiet down, Mrs. Day." Anna looked at Salvatore and rolled her eyes.

Lucia began babbling the second she saw them. Salvatore held her face in both hands. "Tutto bene, amore mio," he said. "I return. Always, I return." Lucia clutched his hands, kissing them, murmuring.

"What's she saying?" Anna asked.

"Who knows? She worry. All the time, she worry."

When they'd lost their daughter, their little Anna, Salvatore was sure it would break her. By then they lived down the block from the store in a bigger apartment, the boys sharing one bedroom, he and Lucia the other. Anna slept in the hallway like Angelo once had.

When she got sick, Lucia moved her into their room. It happened so quickly. One day she cried for Salvatore to carry her up the stairs, her legs bruised like she'd banged them on the monkey bars at the park. Within weeks she was gone, nothing anyone could do, the doctors useless, grim, like stone.

Anna was their miracle, arriving as she did after the war and the deaths of his father and brothers in Italy, after three additional miscarriages and two babies stillborn, Angelo and Joseph already eleven and seven. Salvatore had almost lost hope there would be another child, that Lucia would ever have the daughter she longed for.

He'd expected Lucia to crumble, like with Matteo. But it was Salvatore who crumbled, barely able to function. His sons attempted to keep the shop afloat, Lucia feeding him, cutting his meat, begging him to take one more bite. He wept uncontrollably, and it was she who held his face in her hands. "Amore mio," she comforted. "She will be waiting for us one day. Anna, Enzo, Matteo, they will all be waiting." She'd gestured to Angelo, scribbling his homework at the kitchen table, sweet Joseph at the sink rinsing the supper plates. "But for now, we live. No?"

He'd gazed into her liquid brown eyes, as he had every day for most of his life, knowing she was right. There was no other choice. They would keep going. They would live.

They sold the shop when Salvatore retired. His sons didn't want it. People replaced their shoes now anyway, tossing them when they needed repair. Everything had changed. He and Lucia moved to Queens, the first floor of Joseph's duplex. They joined a new parish, a Polish priest who understood enough Italian to hear Lucia's confession. Salvatore no longer believed in confession, but he sat in the pew beside Lucia every Sunday, trying to pray.

There were new friends who played cards. Some spoke Italian, others only English, mixed with Polish or Spanish. Mornings, Salvatore sat with the old Puerto Rican man around the corner, in metal lawn chairs outside his garage, discussing, debating the state of the neighborhood, the city, the country. Their youngest grandchildren were already in college, but Joseph's girls visited often enough. Everyone gathered for birthdays and holidays, Kathryn and Lucia cooking big Italian feasts. Life was good. Salvatore would have been happy if it ended there. But Lucia started forgetting. Her legs went. Then his heart.

"Why doesn't Mrs. Mili walk?" the girl, Anna, asked, helping Salvatore back to his chair.

"She stay inside. No church, no shop." Salvatore spread his hands. "Then she no walk at all. The doctors say she is lazy." His eyes narrowed. "My wife is never lazy."

"That sucks." Anna frowned. "You've been married forever, huh?"

"Yes, forever." Salvatore sniffed. "But you, how long you stay with the boyfriend that make you cry?"

"Good question." Anna frowned. "I'll leave the rope off, but no getting up. I'll come back after dinner to put you to bed."

"I stay," he said. "I promise."

He heard the tray cart, and an orderly stuck his head in the door, tall, pale skin and small eyes, a photo ID pinned to his navy scrubs. "Table for two?" he announced. As though it was the funniest joke, and he didn't repeat it every night. He set Lucia's tray on her table.

"Bring me her plate." Salvatore gestured. "I cut the meat, put butter on her potatoes the way she like."

"I'll do it." The man popped the lid off and started to cut the chicken. "Umm, looks good."

He was a nice boy, this man, a good boy to take the time. He held out Lucia's fork and she took it, smiling, mumbling, half Italian, half God knows what. "You're so far away," he observed. "Why don't you two sit together, at least for dinner?"

"She make a mess. She drive me crazy." Salvatore laughed so the man would understand he wasn't completely serious.

The orderly nodded emphatically. "Dude, no one likes a food fight." He delivered Salvatore's tray, blowing Lucia a kiss.

Salvatore watched Lucia eat her potatoes with gusto. He picked up his chicken breast and took a small bite. It was too hard, most nights, cutting his own meat, but he found if he asked them to bring him Lucia's meal to cut, they generally did it for her. He made do, rarely hungry. He ate to stay strong, to care for Lucia however he could.

Sometimes they did put Lucia and Salvatore's chairs together, the nurses who didn't know better. But Lucia liked to watch the hallway, see what was coming, while he preferred looking out at the sky, the trees. She cried more when Salvatore sat beside her. As though she thought he might fix this situation they found themselves in, the way they'd always counted on each other to fix whatever broke in their lives.

All those years Lucia ran the house. Salvatore was the one out in the world while Lucia hunkered down at home, even when they'd lived at Joseph's. Everyone needed their own space. Especially here.

"You didn't eat much."

He'd nodded off. Anna stood before him, hands on hips. "I eat enough." Salvatore took off his glasses and rubbed his face.

Anna walked him to the toilet. While he sat, she got Lucia ready, changing her diaper, calling the orderly in to help transfer her onto the bed. When Lucia was tucked in, Anna took out his dentures, holding the basin for him to rinse and spit. She helped him pull on his pajamas, and handed him a warm, wet washcloth for his face and hands, all while he sat on the toilet. "I hear tomorrow is shower day."

He gave her the washcloth and took the towel, eyebrows raised. "Yippee." She rewarded him with a deep belly laugh, a sound so lovely Salvatore's smile spilled into his eyes.

She laid his slippers on the floor. "These were across the room." They walked out of the bathroom and Salvatore sank down on his bed. Anna plucked off the slippers. "I'll put them under the nightstand. Hopefully they won't get lost again."

He attempted to lift his legs onto the bed, but in the end Anna helped, propping pillows against his back and between his knees. She secured the siderails on both beds, carefully pushing Lucia's towards his. The siderails clinked together, Salvatore snatching his hand away so it wouldn't get pinched.

It was not yet dark. The wind was picking up, and the window rattled softly. "Buenas noches." Anna pecked Salvatore's forehead. "Sleep tight, Mr. Mili." She picked up the soiled laundry from the floor and flicked off the light.

"It's Milione," he whispered into the air, knowing she was already gone. "Salvatore Milione." He wove his arm through the railing toward his wife. Lucia reached out and clasped his hand, holding it close against her chest.

Book, Escape, Sanctuary

Lesley Finn

Rigel 2023 Winner

I have no memories of my mother reading during my childhood. I cannot recall her sitting at my bedside with an open storybook in her lap, her chafed hands turning a page, the words of another carried by her voice. Nor can I recall a moment from those years when I came into a room to find her with a book, reading to herself, for herself.

But my mother has a memory of reading, and I am in it. She remembers pushing me on the swing of the neighborhood playground while reading Colleen McCullough's *The Thorn Birds*. I was two, maybe three. Her left hand pushed me in the swing, her right hand held the book. She read and pushed and read and pushed until her friend interrupted with the news that the swing my mother was pushing was empty, and had been for some time.

My memories of my mother do not include memories of her reading because they instead feature her most habitual actions: sweeping, wiping, vacuuming. Decades would pass before I understood why she emptied the trash when there wasn't more than a single tissue in it. Why we left the house only to return minutes later so she could check the door was locked. Why there was no time for reading. In my childhood, these were the realities I accepted.

That day on the playground with *The Thorn Birds*, in the rhythmic action of pushing me on a swing, the obsessions and compulsions that usually clamored in my mother's mind quieted, and the words of the book provided sanctuary. She had, for a handful of minutes, escaped.

And so had I.

Other than reading, my most habitual action as a child was moving around the items and furniture in my room. When I was very small I only rearranged stuffed animals and toys, but as the years passed I became ambitious. My room was only big enough to hold a twin bed, a small chest of drawers, and a desk; a single window overlooked the neighborhood playground. Though there were only so many possible configurations, I felt an acute need to reinvent and reestablish the arrangement, at least once every few weeks. Changing the furniture was claiming my space as mine, a space where I could escape, a space where I could read. I hoarded these spaces where I could hide and be alone with a book, and from which I would always emerge feeling recentered, calm. Outside of the house, I went to the low branches of the neighbor's weeping cherry tree, or the cluster of pines at the end of the street. I don't remember where I went to the day I escaped from the swing, but I suspect it was to a place like this. I was too young to read then, but not for long.

The association between rooms and reading meets poetically in the word stanza, Italian for 'room.' One way of looking at a poem is as a group of connected rooms where the mind can retreat to and reflect. But in any piece of writing words and phrases can build another reality, a sanctuary. In this logic, novels are sprawling houses, filled with hidden pockets of solitude. Books are places where we can escape our cycles of thinking and being, and, in doing so, meet ourselves anew.

The Thorn Birds was a house my mother didn't have to clean. It was a house that freed her of domestic responsibility, of the demands of parenting, a house where she could get lost in and escape the cycle of ritualistic acts that dominated her mental health. It was a sanctuary for her, just as it was for me then, and just as the book is for me now.

The writer Anne Elliott offers a framework for thinking about sanctuary. She does so in the scope of fiction, as a tool for developing character, but I see her idea of sanctuary spilling beyond the room of the page into the room of the reader. Maybe it is easier to think of my mother's life as it intertwined with my own as a storyline. For us, escape was sanctuary, and escape came in the shape of a book.

Of the many features Elliott delineates, one is that a sanctuary is a place "removed from a danger that is otherwise constant." To a woman like my mother — a woman, that is, with obsessive-compulsive disorder — danger took many forms. The threat of dirt and harm, to name two; a toddler with a tendency to escape and hide, to name another. I do not take it lightly that a book once helped to remove my mother from these constants. I often wonder if I became a writer because I internalized, at a young age, that books could free people.

When she tells the story of *The Thorn Birds* and the playground, my mother laughs. "Can you imagine what an idiot I looked like?" She laughs because nothing bad happened, though the shame of what could have must haunt her, as it would any mother. I tell her I don't think she looked like an idiot. I tell her how I tried and failed to read books when my kids were small and begged to be pushed in swings. I tell her it was a good thing that she was so engrossed in the book, and I tell her that the other mothers on the playground were probably jealous. I am trying to say, *You should feel no shame. Celebrate your escape.* I want to ask, *What was it in the book that swept you away?*

What does your sanctuary look like? But we do not have conversations like this. We converse superficially; at best, through subtext.

We do not talk about her OCD. After sharing the news of diagnosis in her fifties, for two decades and counting she has never mentioned it again, as if the diagnosis made the condition disappear. We do not talk about it even when, on visits, the OCD is in plain sight. We do not talk about it, and to cope I practice erasure. When I see her cleaning the clean dish I just took out of the cupboard, I pretend I don't see what she is doing. Sometimes, when I think I am feeling kind, I say, "Thank you." But framing the compulsion in this way is a form of erasure too.

I have never read *The Thorn Birds*, but I have erased it.

Not all erasure is problematic. Erasure can offer a way of seeing, a choice, when it feels like the story in front of you is fixed.

In March 2020 I dreamt of the playground swing, of my mother reading that book — of her memory, as told to me. I had just completed a yearlong diary in which I recorded my dreams and was fascinated by what the subconscious continued to kick up night after night. I decided, upon waking after that particular dream, to order a copy of the book that so curiously connected my mother to me.

All knew was that the novel was a bestseller and a family saga, and that a miniseries of the same title aired on American television in the early 1980s, when I was in elementary school. And that the book had been a source of escape for both of us.

On the first page I saw the name of my daughter — it is the name given to one of the character's dolls, a minor coincidence, but perhaps not. Perhaps the name passed through my mother's body as she read the book, into me as she pushed me on that swing. Perhaps that name reverberated in my body, etched into my muscles with each pump of her arm. Perhaps my mother wrote the name in me, and I remembered. Flipping through the book's pages, I found my son's name too. How much else of me could I trace to the novel's words, sentences, paragraphs? Seeing the synchronicities, though, my instinct wasn't to keep reading. Reading the book for the story seemed somehow evasive and overly direct. Our lives were marked not by telling and by linear story, but by chance and indirection.

Instead of reading, I took out a marker and covered all the words on the novel's page except my daughter's name. Don't worry, it was a cheap, paperback copy. I had never done anything like that before, and I wish I could tell you where this instinct came from; all I can tell you is what happened, and what came from it.

Perhaps drawing on the page was both an escape and a way to go deeper. Erasure, the practice of blacking out, covering up, or erasing preexisting text to create new meaning, is a practice of escape. It allows the writer to choose one meaning over another, *this* arrangement of words instead of *that* arrangement of words. In March 2020, housebound from the pandemic, I could transcend the walls around me and escape into the house of the book. I could choose one house over another.

I say I haven't read *The Thorn Birds*, but I think of this practice of erasure, which I continue to do with the book nearly three years later, as a way of reading. I am searching for the story beneath the story that my mother's mind was drawn to, the words and images that spoke to her and her alone. No one reads the same book; we take in different variations of meaning and significance. There is the plot, and then there is the book we hold in our memories, which no one but us can access.

I am not escaping into the rooms of the book to hide. I am trying to find the room in the book where my mother and I can meet.

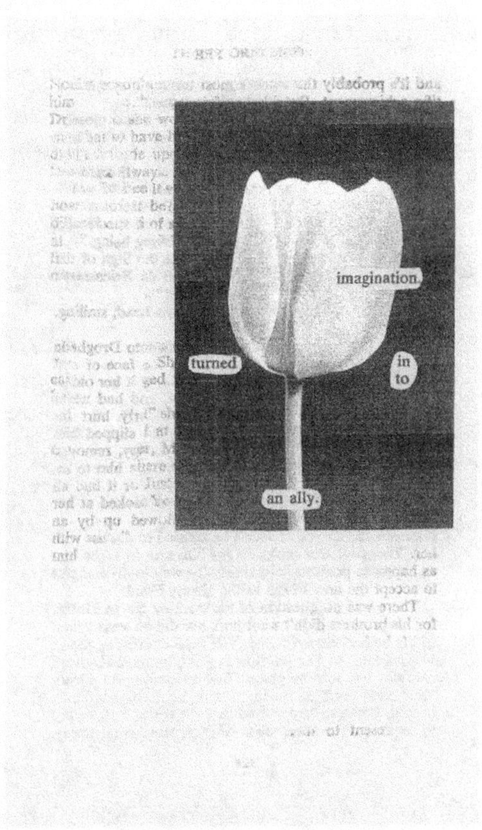

For years after its identification in the seventeenth century, OCD was considered a sign of insanity, which perhaps was an improvement over its original association with satanic possession. Either way, people with OCD were seen to have uncontrollable, morally suspicious urges, like the blurting out of blasphemous, inappropriate thoughts.

I would like to know my mother's blasphemous thoughts.

Elliott, in her definition of sanctuary, observes that it "is a place where the masks and armor of everyday life can be removed." Did my mother read *The Thorn Birds*, feel the lift of masks and armor, and think:

> I wish I had no child to swing.
> I wish I could run away to Australia.
> Who wouldn't like to fuck a priest?

It wasn't until the nineteenth century that the insanity designation for OCD shifted to neurosis, and that delusion was understood to be different from obsession. The difference: "insight was preserved" in obsessions, whereas delusions were, accordingly, devoid of insight. That is, we are aware, or have the ability to be aware of, our obsessions. Then along came Freud, who suggested those with OCD actively practiced "reaction formation," a process of "adopting traits that were the opposite of the feared impulses."

If Freud was right, my mother's traits, the traits of the indefatigable stay-at-home mom, spotless homemaker, unceasingly supportive wife, and conflict-avoidant peacekeeper, stood in opposition to what?

It would only make sense that my mother secretly desired to be a childless single woman, with a thriving career, and a filthy, cluttered house.

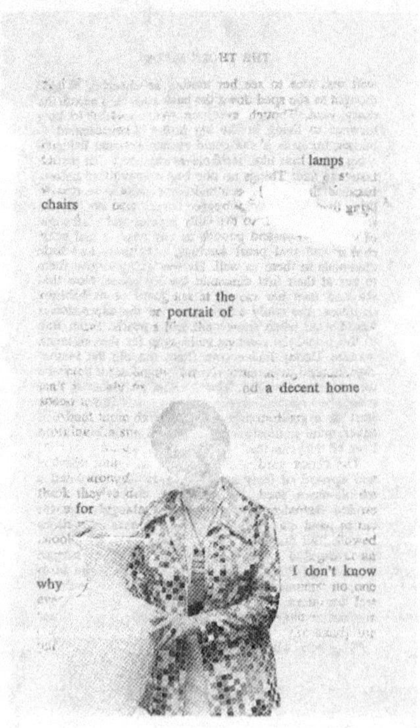

As is the case with many mental health conditions, the current prevailing psychology has a more compassionate approach to OCD, but the framework of the past is hard to shake. Along with the "insanity with insight" take, there were physicians who labeled OCD "a disease of the emotions" resulting from a "weakness of character." Pierre Janet, who is credited with our modern understanding of the condition, held that obsessions resulted from a "defect in 'the function of the real.'"

I remember being a restless eight-year-old running into the kitchen to get a glass of orange juice, wanting nothing more than a quick drink between episodes on a Saturday morning cartoon binge. Hasty with my pour, I spilled juice on the counter, and when I tried to clean it up knocked the juice carton onto the floor. My mother materialized from nowhere, roaring, wailing, her face red with anger and wet with tears. "How could you?" she screeched. "I just cleaned the floor . . . how could you?"

What was real for my mother: a clean floor, and then a floor coated with sticky, spreading juice. The reality of the house was that she was the person who cleaned up, but this reality was not all her own doing. On a Saturday morning, my father could have helped, but he didn't. There were so many unstated expectations in our house, and one was that my mother — who for far too long I interpreted as all mothers, and all women — was the one to clean up. Obsessions result from a defect in the function of the real, but who said the function of the real wasn't defective from the start? I have felt pushed to the edge of madness when I see the structures and conditioning that encouraged and have ensured my husband's career over mine. The barely existent paternity leave that allowed my husband to return to work and left me looking after our firstborn, despite the fact that only a year before I had been earning more money and never agreed to assume the sole caregiver role. That was the function of the real, and it was and remains colossally problematic — defective, if you ask me. And I have, in tears, roaring, on more than one occasion, said to my husband, "How could you?"

I was dumbstruck by my mother's reaction, but eventually helped her clean, all the while aware that what I was doing was not enough. There was a deeper anger in her, a space that I could only witness from the outside, a wilderness she seemed to roam unhappily in. I was confused by it, and frustrated I didn't know how to make it disappear.

If "a sanctuary is a place where the character can experience emotions naturally," as Elliott suggests, it might be tempting to think of the kitchen that day as my mother's sanctuary. But that would be wrong. Even on the best days the kitchen put my mother's emotions through a meat grinder. The crumbs. The half-empty glasses. The mustard-crusted butter knife. I'm not sure what "naturally" means when we are talking about women in kitchens, just as I'm not sure what reality means for most women either.

When I think about the kitchen that day, the orange juice spill, my mother's rage, I wish I had thought more creatively in the moment. I wish I had had the imagination to fetch her a book, to guide her to sofa, to insist she read. Or even simpler: the imagination to hug her, to agree that the spill was an annoying and unfair thing.

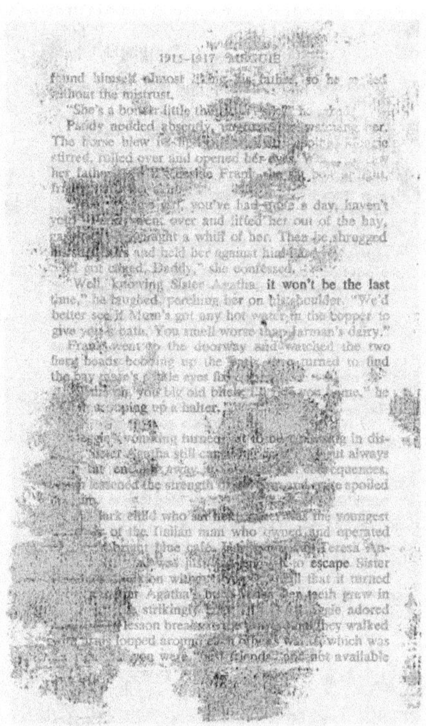

OCD shows no particular gender affinity, but it's certainly possible that OCD, like depression and other conditions, is perceived differently according to gender roles. In my family's case, my mother's OCD could at times be invisible, because it aligned with social codes of what it meant to be a good mother. It was, in that way, "natural." The house was clean. My father was unbothered by domestic duties and could focus on his career. And I was unburdened by chores, free to move my furniture around and read. If my mother had insanity with insight, I would call the conditions around my mother observation without insight.

OCD for a woman of my mother's generation, born in the 1940s, enabled a special kind of gender entrapment. She was expected to have children and an immaculate home, conditions on which her OCD would thrive. As a family, we were, in a gross, craven way, benefitting from her condition. My father likes to joke that my mom's favorite pastime is wiping down the counter two times in a row, that the second time brings her so much pleasure. As if it is her art. As if the kitchen is indeed her sanctuary. I struggle to recall seeing him with a dishcloth in his hand.

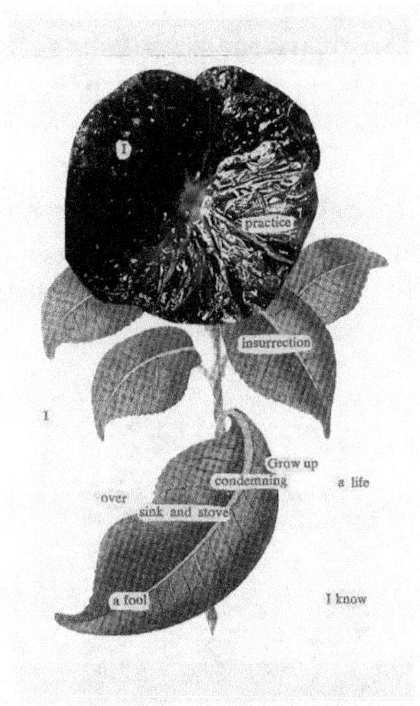

Sanctuary, as Elliott defines it, is a place where "creativity, epiphany, intimacy, or risk-taking is possible," but every one of these endeavors is blocked by OCD. The condition locks the sufferer in routines of familiarity, free of the risk that creates growth and knowledge. Epiphany has no room in the tight spaces of obsession and compulsion, and the only intimacy is with the repetition of ritual.

But ritual, when it creates self-knowledge and community, can be positive, nourishing. And so I am making a ritual out of reading but not reading McCullough's novel. To understand my mother, our shared past, I need to go back to the playground, back to the swing, to one of my mother's hands on my back, the other on that book. That moment — and that book — was and is where creativity, epiphany, intimacy, and risk-taking are possible for us.

I am reading *The Thorn Birds* to create a sanctuary for my mother and me. It is a room like no other I've rearranged, existing on the page and in shared memories, and it doesn't look like reading. I erase and cover lines at random, see what the remaining words evoke, and make intuitive collages in response: pictures of the horses my mother never learned to ride, the antiques she collected but that got donated in move after move. I follow no aesthetic constraint other than keeping the words on the page in the order they appear. Sometimes I blindly press paint on the page until single words remain: once, this happened with the word playground. It is as though the book is reminding me that it has always known us, connected us, and that it sees a path forward. That path, I believe, isn't a conversation. It's a stack of pages — infused with empathy, confession, and possibility — that I can hand to her. The book as I am remaking it is both childhood witness and adult reflection. I don't know that I could hold both in the same space without it.

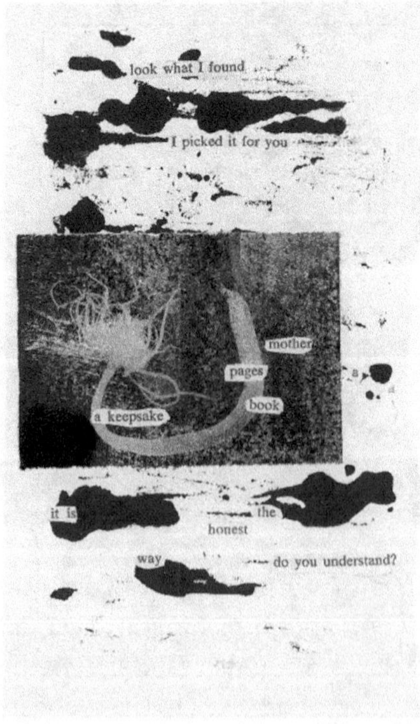

Choice, especially risk-taking choice, can be a challenge to people with OCD: there is a palpable fear of making the "wrong" choice, of disrupting an established equilibrium, of detouring from the routine and the known. Choose this or that, *or or or* — the options and their consequences overwhelm. I saw it in my mother every time she bought lipstick: she would take me with her to the store determined to buy a new shade and leave with a replica of what she always wore, filling her makeup drawer with sameness. But *or* can be freeing too, as is the case with the rearranged room, the reimagined page, and this is what I am seeking in my erasure of *The Thorn Birds*. *Or* can be an improvisational cousin of *yes and* — the creative *or* that seeks the epiphany in chance. The word *or* is embedded in the book's title after all.

Erasure in the way I am doing it is, I hope, escape with insight. This time instead of running away from my mother, I am trying to run to her.

Moon

Irene Blair Honeycutt

Geminga 2023 Finalist

Though some have
Called you *corpse*
You are alive to me
No matter how
Ghostly you appear
Early mornings
The sky gauzy

Riverside, Dubuque, IA Series

/ Christopher Paul Brown

Geminga 2023 Finalist

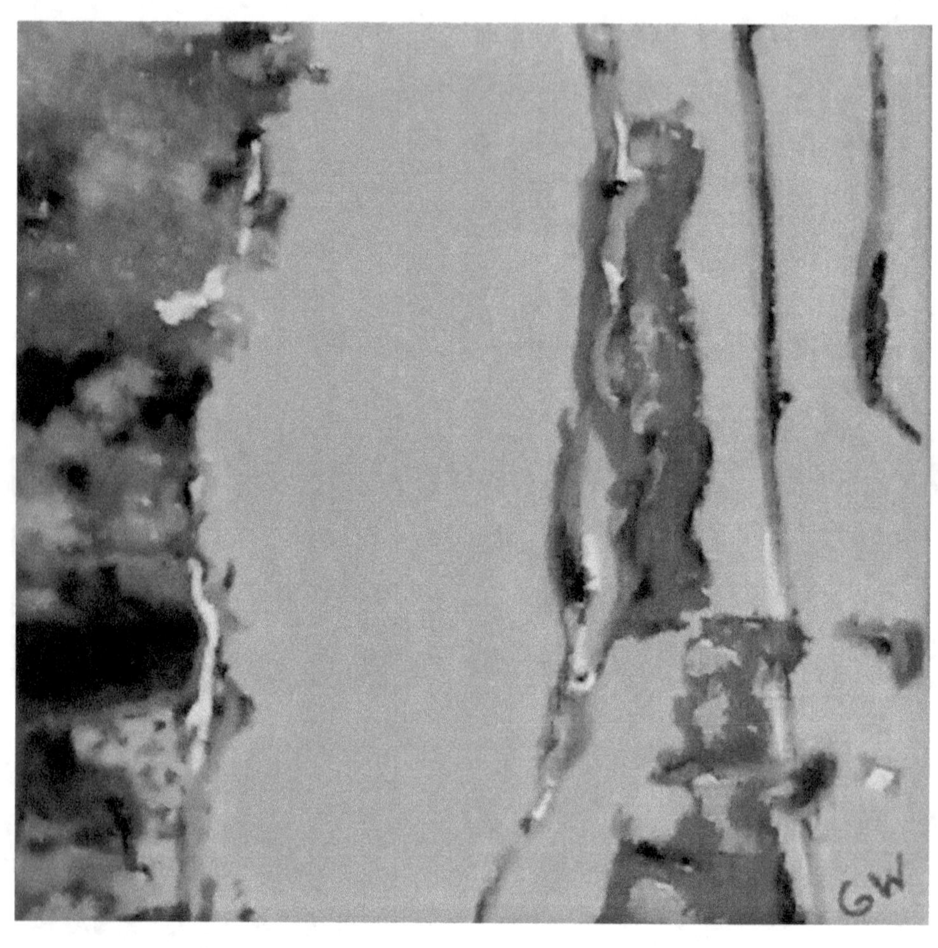

RUST / GINNA WILKERSON

GEMINGA 2023 FINALIST

I Can Tell You

Kyle Gardner

Geminga 2023 Finalist

I could tell you. I could tell you what it feels like to watch the sun's fire go dark. I could tell you what it sounds like when the wind dies and the only sound you hear ringing in your ears are words you wish you could've said when you had the chance and words you wished you had never heard to begin with. I could tell you what Icarus saw in the clouds drowning in the sunlight, and the songs Orpheus sang in the blackness of Hell. I could tell you. But I won't. They are for me.

Regarding your workplace

Ben Elliott

Geminga 2023 Finalist

Quantuscumque onus imponatur tam immerite in te,
 ecce susurrum spei tecum adero opperiens.

Howsoever great a burden is imposed,
 so unfairly, upon you,
know this: I will be there,
 waiting with you for a whisper of hope.

WEB / SUSAN DAMBROFF

GEMINGA 2023 FINALIST

HOW THE GIANTESS BECAME SMALL

/ AMY MARQUES

GEMINGA 2023 FINALIST

AND BLOOD THE NEXT DAY

BRENDAN STRAUBEL

GEMINGA 2023 FINALIST

Coming home late, I stopped to watch the salmon run. The water was dropping and clear. I made some half-hearted casts. But the fish were old now, trailing their bloodless flesh and gunmetal skins upstream. Upstream, in the warm twilight, like rotting, ragged flags.

You first felt the baby move that morning. Like butterfly wings, you said. Underwater.

I got home after dark, spooned up close, spreading my fingers against your belly. Your breathing soft and regular in the dark. Until . . . a soft swirl: a Coho's slow roll at the eddyline.

Or butterfly wings. Underwater.

And then nothing. Nothing at all.

Leftover Summer Somnolence

Katrina Lemaire

Geminga 2023 Finalist

You were a whisper of late summer sunsets
left behind a canopy of willows
the kind of midnight moon
that woke the eye of dawn
when stars slept

—*leftover summer somnolence*

RESTORATION / JUAN GALLO

GEMINGA 2023 FINALIST

PLUMERIA

HELEN WU

GEMINGA 2023 BEST OF POETRY

three times now you've left
plumeria on my step
this time, I'll listen

CANOPY

KIM DOWNEY

GEMINGA 2023 BEST OF CREATIVE NONFICTION

Don't let the eyelets and white ruffles and four posts fool you: I was no princess in a tower. No one hid me from the world.

The white berries on the bush in the backyard were poisonous. On the news, murders and exploding mountains. Then my father's brain bled. And something happened in the woods that night. "You know," said my friend when I asked, her dark eyes flashing.

No one hid the world from me. What existed between me and falling meteors? Only a roof and a ceiling and a flimsy cotton canopy between me and the unpredictable sky.

What Is a Mouth

EZAM

Geminga 2023 Best of Graphic Novel

But as the days wore on...,
I became less and less sure of the world -

And my place in it.

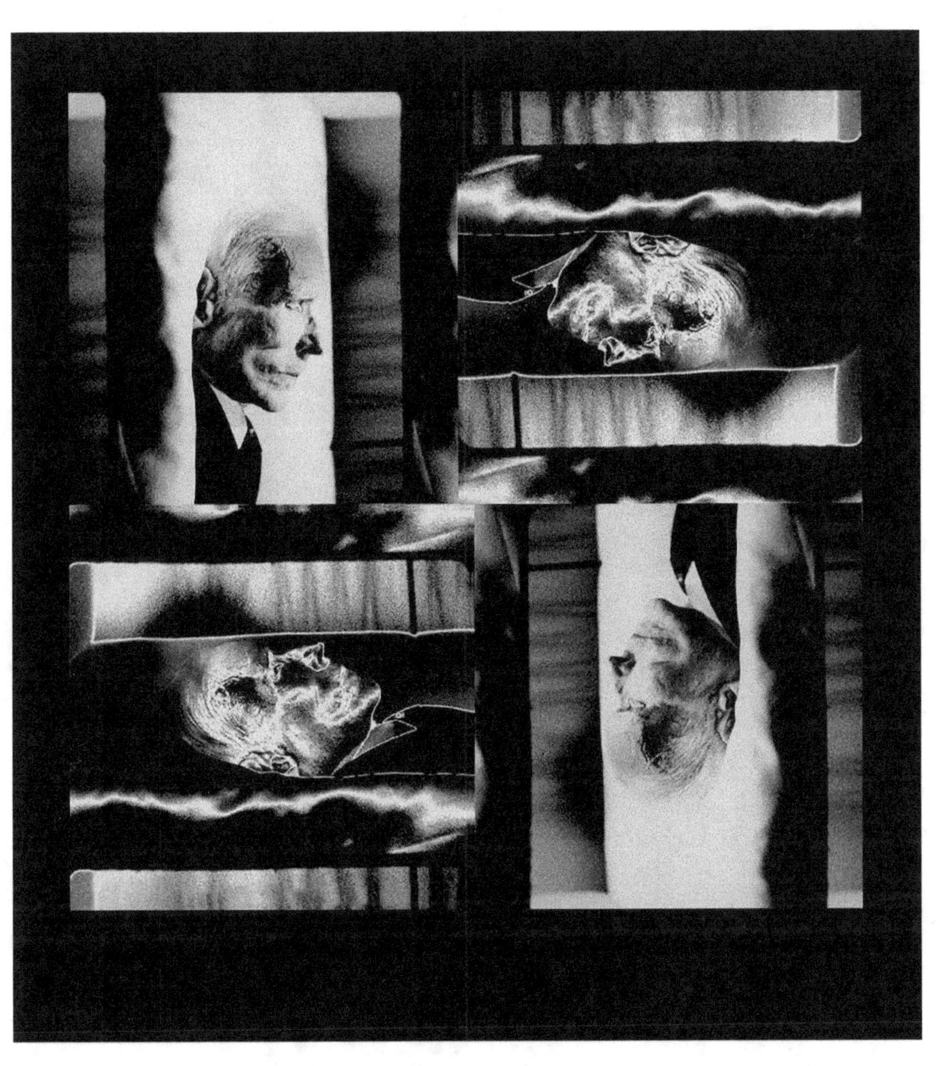

Death Portrait of Pappoo

/ Peter Chechopoulos

Geminga 2023 Best of Art

THE WEATHER CIRCUS

OSHOTO ROWAN

GEMINGA 2023 WINNER

(from a dream)

Bedraggled as old crows, they gather in their black clothes, and the sky begins to darken. Clouds as grey and old as summer thunderstorms, but greenish tinged. A hurricane coming.

Some sing, as they erect the tents. An old dirge: an elegy of thunder; of the cold sea and dark ground; the relentless drive of the mountains pushing their fingers into the secret earth to arise, bejeweled. They sing, black clothes, faces shadowed, the songs from their throats dark.

Silence falls; a wind picks up. The clouds pace them.

Wherever they go, the smell of rain always follows.

WOODCUTTER

DANIELLE STONEHIRSCH

INCEPTION 2023 FINALIST

Once upon a time, a woodcutter lived at the edge of a lonely forest. The woodcutter had a wife as lovely as the summer sun setting over the snow-capped trees. They were kind-hearted, though poor, and were known to provide aid to the occasional fleeing princess or lost traveler. The woodcutter and his wife had a daughter as beautiful as the angels of Heaven. She grew up in the cottage at the edge of the forest and married a miller's son and had a daughter, and their daughter had a daughter, and her daughter had a daughter, and her daughter had a daughter, and her daughter had a daughter, and her daughter had a daughter named Angel who worked at Home Depot in the lumber department cutting planks of wood in half for over-zealous do it yourselfers.

The Home Depot was located on forest land that had been razed by developers trying to make money in a quiet upstate town where Angel lived a quiet upstate life. She was neither rich nor poor, making minimum wage at Home Depot and filling in the rest working evenings at local shop Create! helping seven-year-olds at birthday parties paint ceramic mugs their parents could display until such time it was appropriate to tell their children their art was all crap and finally throw it away.

BUZZKILL

LEILA BATATIAN SPRINGER

INCEPTION 2023 FINALIST

June 2050

Venice, California

Spin off the lip of the biggest bowl in the skate park, witching hour of 4 a.m., braids whipping in the yellow drizzle, park lights flickering at half bright, gates locked but I nicked the code right out of Sally Security's head. Drop down the bowl and hurtle across, crouching low, the whoosh of my wheels the only sound. Flick the rain off my face and burp the edge, kick to the wall and jump it. No one here but me, so no staring, no whispering *Is that her?* Pulling up the photos and yep, it's me, "The Campus Killer." The lack of originality is depressing.

That's not even the problematic bit, that I killed someone. The problematic bit is, I would do it again. I *will* do it again. I won't be able not to.

Unless something stops me.

Sally Security's due for her next check in fifteen, where she will kick me out. Highlight of her night but of course she doesn't know I know. I know way too many things I shouldn't and wouldn't and it's a fucked-up deal, a fucking toxic bomb fucking stirring up my brain, making me fucking psychic of all fucking things, ruining my fucking life.

Twirl one three-sixty after another at the bottom of the bowl, dim yellow lights spinning over my starvation-dizzy head, looking up at the sky like an ice skater at the Olympics.

Breathe, Lola. Breathe. Ten months — fourteen, tops — and it'll all be over.

A DREAM OF TIBET / BILL SCHULZ

INCEPTION 2023 FINALIST

The Devil in the Details

Taylor J. Morley

Inception 2023 Finalist

Sure. God and I hadn't been on speaking terms for a while, but I guess I hadn't realized exactly where we were at. I thought we were just ignoring each other again, so imagine my surprise when the devil sat down next to me at the bus stop. He wasn't smoking a cigarette, dressed in black, or sporting two pointy horns. All things considered, he looked different than expected.

He hadn't dramatically appeared from the shadows with a burst of fire or a puff of smoke. He'd braved the rain, just like I had, and taken refuge at the pavilion where the bus had been due to stop a half hour ago.

Without a doubt, the bus's punctuality, or lack thereof, was his fault. He removed a pack of watermelon gum, popped a piece in his mouth, and extended another to me while smiling warmly. I took it and chewed it. But that didn't mean a thing. He outstretched his hand to me and gave me a fake name. While I wasn't thrilled about making his acquaintance, I was a little intimidated by the idea of offending such a being. I racked my brain as he made awkward small talk, complimenting my choice of shoes. Why was he here?

I'd made my fair share of questionable choices. I'd committed some actions that were legally frowned upon, stained my hands more than my fair share, and snatched a few things that weren't quite mine. But coming for my soul himself? Really?

Deus in Machina

Kay Suz

Inception 2023 Finalist

The walls in this part of the prison were the wrong color. They were clean and shiny, and unquestionably the wrong color. Every other area was painted a dirty mint green. To keep the prisoners calm, they said. To keep them under control. Someone had told him that green makes time seem shorter, the rooms larger. And that it promotes harmony. It didn't really work like that in a place like this. He didn't know if the men there felt calmer, but they definitely all hated that color. And it didn't serve its purpose yesterday when the one they called Preacher decided he'd had enough of Coyote's bullshit and put a sharpened stylus through his throat. No color in the world could reduce the number of body bags leaving this place every week.

But this hallway, leading him to his long-awaited freedom, was more of a buttery yellow. Maybe to prepare parolees for the life they were about to return to. No, not return. Begin. After more than sixteen years, it would be a new life for him. A new world. It had changed, and then changed again, but not in the way he had wanted. And even though the counselors had spent all those hours talking to him in their soothing tones, he wasn't prepared for it. He knew it would still be alien and strange and wrong. It was not the world he had worked so hard to create before he went in.

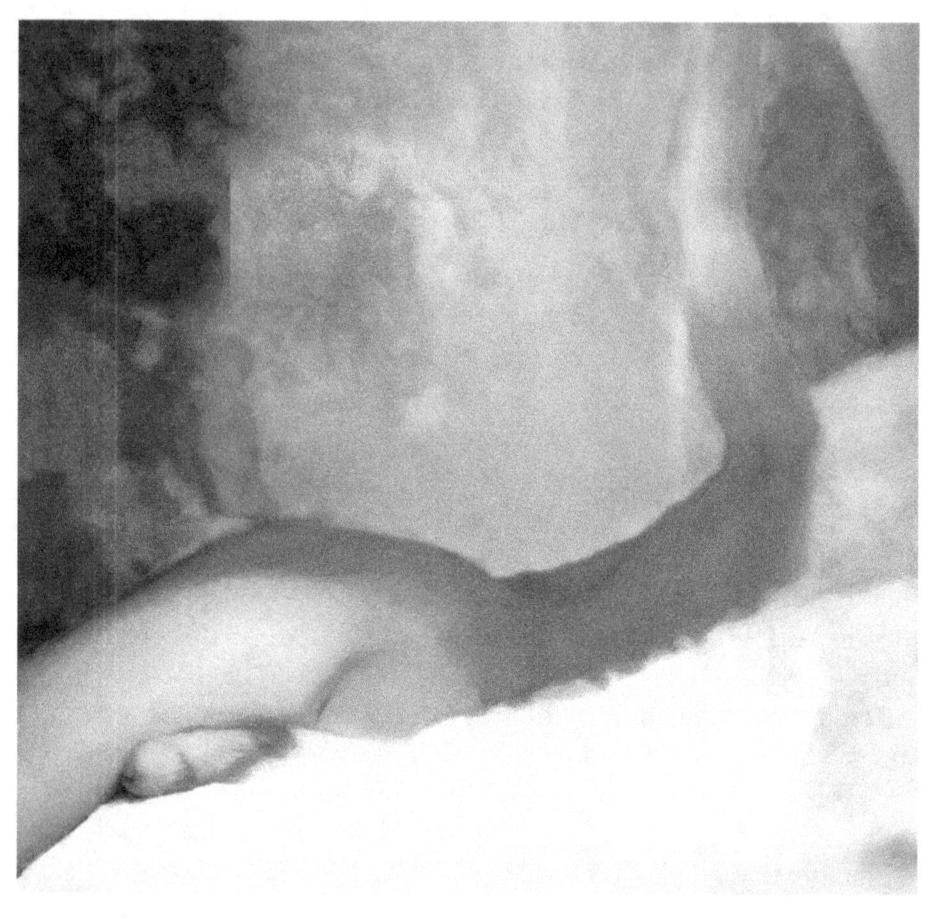

Genesis / Rex Wilder

Inception 2023 Runner-up, Best of Art

GRINDERS AND CREAM

ROBERT HICKSON

INCEPTION 2023 RUNNER-UP, BEST OF FICTION

Lying on the living room couch one late spring evening, the sound of gunfire and explosions gently washing over her, mist like, from the latest Netflix action movie playing in the den, Bunny Naples, cell phone in hand, searched online for a new pair of athletic shoes. This year is different, she told herself. Her oldest son was getting married in the fall, and after looking at herself in the mirror, decided to get in shape. A pound here, maybe two there, better make that three; nothing too strenuous, the less sweat the better. Necessity is the mother of reduction, as the TV commercials shouted.

Shopping online was for Bunny, like for millions of other people lying on their couches this particular spring evening, tantalizing, like an apple in the Garden of Eden. A click click here, and a click click there, here a click, there a click and the next morning, Bunny, and millions like her, would be awakened to the sound of delivery trucks backup alarms sounding as the trucks backed into driveways, followed by a quick ring of the doorbell, letting the purchasers inside know that day's Edenic apple had arrived. By this point Bunny's dog, Spliffy, would be barking by the glass paneled front door; her husband, Jeremy, would be cursing in a long-forgotten tongue, and the morning would begin with a little cloud over said garden. Maybe just one click tonight, thought Bunny.

NIGHTWALK / BILL SCHULZ

INCEPTION 2023 WINNER

CONTRIBUTORS

Dan Alter has published poems widely in journals including *Field*, *Fourteen Hills*, *Pank*, and *Zyzzyva*. His collection, *My Little Book of Exiles*, published in 2022 by Eyewear Press, won the poetry prize for the 2022 Anne and Robert Cowan Writer's Awards. He lives in Berkeley with his wife and daughter where he makes his living as an IBEW electrician. www.danalter.net

Nathan Bachman is a public-school teacher in central Ohio. Bachman's fiction has appeared in many publications, but most recently in Terrain.org, *Hobart*, and *The Flagler Review*.

Yakir Ben-Moshe, an Israeli poet of Iraqi descent, won the Prime Minister's Prize for Literature in 2012. He has published four books of poetry and one of children's literature. He lives with his wife and children in Tel Aviv, where he is the Literary Editor of the Bialik House, as well as a teacher of creative writing.

Jack Bordnick's sculptures and photography incorporate surrealistic, mythological and magical imagery — often with whimsical overtones — aimed at provoking our experiences and self-reflections. The predominant imagery deals with facial expressions of living and "non-living" beings, and things that speak to us in their own languages. The mixed media assemblages have been assembled, disassembled and reassembled, becoming abstractions. Jack has been a designer and design director for the past twenty years.

Christopher Paul Brown is known for his exploration of the unconscious and the serendipitous. His first photography sale was to the Standard Oil Company of Indiana. He earned a BA in Film from Columbia College Chicago in 1980. Brown was born in Dubuque, Iowa and now resides in North Carolina.

Cristina Bryan has worked as a professional editor for thirty-five years, and ran a small regional book publisher, Barclay Bryan Press. She is now retired. *Henricus* is her first novel.

J Carraher was formally trained as an anthropologist and medical sociologist and currently works as a forensic examiner in California. Raised in Montana, she has made her home in the San Francisco Bay Area for thirty years. She lives on a small apple orchard in Sebastopol.

Peter Chechopoulos has worked as a teacher, photographer, and director at Chicago State University, Jane Addams Hull House, McHenry County College, After School Matters, and Latino Youth Alternative High School, and as a commercial photographer. His documentary and fine-art photos, films and videos have been shown and published by *Chicago Defender*, *Chicago Magazine*, *Main Photographic Workshops Annual Awards* 1986 & 1987, *Camera Arts,* and Illinois State Museum. Chechopoulos has won numerous honors and awards and his work is in many Collections, including the Library of Congress National Film Collection and IL Institute of Design Archives IIT.

Martha Clarkson's photography can be found at NYC4pa, *Lightbox Photography Gallery F-Stop Magazine*, Black Box Gallery, *Sunspot Magazine*, LensCulture, Light, Space, and Time Gallery, *Ours Photography magazine*, *CALYX*, and *Junto Magazine.* www.marthaclarkson.com

Armed with an MFA from Boston University, **Cynthia Close** plowed her way through several productive careers in the arts, including instructor in drawing and painting, Dean of Admissions at The Art Institute of Boston, founder of ARTWORKS Consulting, and president of Documentary Educational Resources. She now claims to be a writer. To support this claim, she is a contributing editor for *Documentary Magazine* and writes regularly about art, cinema, and culture for, *Artist's Magazine, Art & Object, Pastel Journal, Watercolor Artist, Art New England.*

Jon Cohen lives in Los Angeles with his wife and sixteen-year-old daughter. He is a writer trapped in the body of a music executive. Despite kicking and screaming throughout his successful and reluctant career in music, he's been left with two invaluable gifts: the ability to stay up past his bedtime, and the unswerving desire to get the fuck out of the music biz.

Hardy Coleman lives in "interesting times" within the 3rd Precinct of Minneapolis, MN. He once had two poems published in *Modern Drunkard Magazine* and cooked a meal for both the B 52's and the Rolling Stones.

Michael Cullinane is an emerging writer and a veteran educator presently teaching Broadcast Journalism at a Chicago Public High School. He received his Master's in Digital Storytelling from Loyola University. His fiction recently won first place in the 2023 Slippery Elm contest.

Susan Dambroff is a poet, performer, and teacher who has also just started thinking of her doodles as art. Her poetry chapbooks, *Conversations with Trees* and *A Chair Keeps the Floor Down,* were both published by Finishing Line Press. She performs in the Bay Area in Spoken Duets, a poetic collaboration with Chris Kammler to give voice to the world's massive injustices.

Allison A. deFreese (she/her/ella) is a poet and literary translator. Her translations of Carolina Esses's work appear in *Bellingham Review*, *Eunoia Review*, and *Mantis*. Recent literary translations include María Negroni's *Elegy for Joseph Cornell*, Verónica González Arredondo's *Green Fires of the Spirits*, and Karla Marrufo's *Flame Trees in May*.

Kim Downey is a writer, mother, and pet owner. She lives in British Columbia.

Ben Elliott, originally from Canada, is a grad student in Classics at the University of Georgia. His current interests include John Cassian, Latin poetry, and sculpture, as well as his wonderful family.

Writer and journalist **Carolina Esses** (Buenos Aires, Argentina) has published several books of poems, including *Versiones del paraíso/Variations on Paradise* and *Temporada de invierno/Winter Season* (translation by Allison A. deFreese, forthcoming by Entre Ríos Books). Her poems have been translated into French and appeared in the anthology *Poésie récente d'Argentine, une anthologie possible / Recent Poetry from Argentina: A Possible Anthology*. A literary critic for La Nación, Argentina's leading daily paper, she is also the author of several novels.

EZAM is a reader and librarian from Colorado. She loves comics, especially the weird ones that lodge themselves in the small crannies of your brain. Find her on Instagram @nooshkna.

Lesley Finn writes and makes visual art about the entanglement of narrative, history, and gender. Journals publishing her recent work include *Longreads*, *Atticus Review*, and *Storm Cellar*. Her short stories and essays have been nominated for the Best Small Fictions anthology and the Pushcart Prize. Other honors include serving as Artist-in-Residence for the Connecticut Audubon Society and an Eccles Fellowship at the British Library. Originally from Baltimore, she lives in Connecticut.

Juan Gallo's watercolor was created to show the similarity between love and nature. The two ideas are tied by the different things laid out throughout the environment representing the qualities of growth, decay, death, and rebirth.

Kyle Gardner is a twenty-three-year-old man living in Studio City, California. He's been passionately writing prose and scripts, typically fiction, for six years and is currently working on the production of his short film. When he's not writing or watching films, you can find him waiting tables at a fine-dining supper club for minimum wage.

GJ Gillespie is a collage artist living in a 1928 Tudor Revival farmhouse overlooking Oak Harbor on Whidbey Island. In addition to natural beauty, he is inspired by art history— especially mid-century abstract expressionism like the Northwest

Mystics. Winner of twenty awards, his art has appeared in sixty shows and more than ninety publications, including eleven covers. When he is not making art, he runs his sketchbook company Leda Art Supply.

Maureen D. Hall is a writer/poet, mother of three, and small-town librarian. Her work has appeared in numerous publications including, *Paterson Literary Review*, *Hospital Drive*, *Journal of New Jersey Poets*, *Nursing*, *Avalon*, *American Journal of Nursing*, *Mothering*, *Vineyard Poets*, *Island Quintet*, *Isele Magazine*, *Alma Magazine*, and *Halfway Down the Stairs*. Her poetry has been nominated for a Pushcart Prize. She lives in New England. Twitter: @Maureen_D_Hall; IG: @mdhmv

Marcy Rae Henry is a multidisciplinary artist, una Latina de Los Borderlands and part of the LGBTQ community. She is delighted by tablas, tulips and the theremin. M.R. Henry's writing has received a Chicago Community Arts Assistance Grant, an Illinois Arts Council Fellowship, and a Pushcart Prize nomination. Other writing and visual art appear in *The Columbia Review*, *carte blanche*, *PANK*, *The Southern Review*, *Cauldron Anthology* and *The Brooklyn Review*, among others. DoubleCross Press will publish her chapbook this year.

Robert Hickson works as an instructional assistant in the special education department of a high school in eastern Connecticut.

Irene Blair Honeycutt has published four poetry books, most recently *Beneath the Bamboo Sky* (Main Street Rag 2017). She founded Central Piedmont Community College's Sensoria Arts Festival, which had a twenty-nine-year run. She lives in Indian Trail, NC and is working on her fifth poetry manuscript.

Mark Hurtubise had numerous works published during the 1970s. Then came family, two college presidencies, and CEO of a community foundation. After a four-decade hiatus, he is creating again from the Pacific Northwest. Recently, his poetry, fiction, essays, interviews, and photographs have appeared in *pacificREVIEW*, *Grub Street*, *San Pedro River Review*, *Burningword*, *WhimsicalPoet*, *December*, *Wayne Literary Review*, *North Dakota Quarterly*, *Stanford Social Innovation Review*, *Penumbra*, *Monovisions Black & White Photography*, and *Monochrome*.

Tamar Jacobs' work appears in *Gulf Coast*, *Glimmer Train*, *The Louisville Review*, *New Ohio Review*, *L'Esprit*, *Platform*, and elsewhere. Jacobs' unpublished novel, *A Kind of Music Not a Song*, was a finalist for the Janus Prize awarded by the Chautauqua Institution, and was longlisted for the Nilsen Prize awarded by Southeast Missouri State University Press. She is also a Katherine Anne Porter Fiction Prize winner.

Harry Lee James has been a farmer, soldier, and civil servant, and now lives as a writer and evolving artist sharing a wonderfully entangled workspace with his wife Michelle, who designs and makes jewelry.

Colleen Kam Siu is a poet and artist based in Southern Montana. Her work is inspired by seasonal cycles and shifts in nature that compel transformation. Her poetry has appeared in *Evening Street*, *POETiCA*, *Fahmidan Journal*, *Two Hawks Quarterly*, *Witches Mag*, *Cider Press Review*, and *Devil's Party Press*. You can read and see more of her poetry and art via her recently released chapbook of poetry and paintings, *Elements of Being*, at www.colleenkamsiu.com.

Liam Keller is a technical writer based in Toronto, Canada. He is the recipient of the Meet Me @ 19th Street 2021 First Quarter novel excerpt competition from Arch Street Press. He writes casually, in his spare time, to explore themes of alienation and the surreal in everyday life.

Leslie Kerby's artwork focuses on the social networks and systems that, daily and broadly, impact each of us as individuals. She is particularly interested in networks and systems in moments of significant change. Her work is held in permanent collections at Columbia University, Arkansas State University, and Copelouzos Art Museum, Athens Greece.

Myrth Killingsworth's (she/they) work recently won the tiny journal's climate change contest and was featured in Issue 84 of *The Cafe Irreal*. Killingsworth is an MFA candidate at the Vermont College of Fine Arts, where she serves as Managing Editor and Associate Fiction Editor for the literary magazine *Hunger Mountain*.

Joy Kloman was a tenured associate professor at University of Mississippi, who supervised graduate and undergraduate painting programs and taught drawing in London. She received a Mississippi Arts Commission Individual Artist State Grant, and had work displayed in The Drawing Center Viewing Program & Slide Registry, NY.

Katrina Lemaire is a poet and fiction writer from Ontario, Canada who is currently finishing her degree in English and Creative Writing with a minor in Canadian Studies.

Andrea Lewis' stories, essays, and flash fiction have appeared in many online and print journals including *Prairie Schooner*, *Raleigh Review*, and *Briar Cliff Review*. Her collection of linked stories, *What My Last Man Did*, won the Blue Light Books Prize for fiction and was published by Indiana University Press. She lives in Seattle, WA.

Luann Lewis is the author of the popular *Twisting Time* romance series and other novels and novellas. A Chicago native, she has had short fiction, creative essays, and poetry published online and in print. Her educational video scripts on environmental issues have been produced professionally, and she has had a flash fiction piece performed by Manawaker studios.

Lior Locher is a nonbinary mixed-media artist, mainly working in acrylic and collage and printmaking. After having lived in six countries on four continents and being homeless at some point, they are now based at the English seaside.

Gina Maranto is a prizewinning science writer recently retired from the University of Miami.

Amy Marques grew up between languages and places, and learned from an early age the multiplicity of narratives. She has work published in journals and anthologies, including *Streetcake*, *Bending Genres*, *Gone Lawn*, *Chicago Quarterly*, and *Reservoir Road*. https://amybookwhisperer.wordpress.com

Tyler McCurry is a thirty-three-year-old author from Olathe, Kansas with a passion for food, family and fun, but especially food. A true starving artist.

Kendal McGinnis is a master's student in writing at the University of Illinois in Chicago, where she teaches German and does lots of standup comedy.

Róisín McIntosh is a short-story writer working from under the Blackstairs Mountains in Ireland. She holds an MA in Literature and recently completed a Diploma in Creative Writing. She is currently working on her first short story collection.

Deborah McMillion is an illustrator of ghost stories, graphic books, fine art, postales, Artistamps and zines.

Kyle Mercer's plays have been performed at one-act festivals around the country and as part of a double-bill at the Finborough Theatre in London. He studied with Edward Albee at the University of Houston and is currently trying his hand at fiction, recently completing a collection of literary stories, and is putting the final touches to a mainstream novel.

Taylor J. Morley is a twenty-year-old college student with a passion for writing and storytelling.

Michael Murphy's fiction has featured in *Squawk Back* and *MONO*, his non-fiction in the *Asheville Citizen-Times*, his write-for-hire pablum in myriad feeds, screens, and pulp. While living in London, he wrote an award-winning satirical column for the *Hampstead Village Voice*, eavesdropped on the Tube, and overstayed his welcome at some of the world's most welcoming pubs.

Alex Nodopaka originated last century in Kyiv, Ukraine. He speaks, reads and writes San Franciscan, Parisian, Kievan and Muscovite. Mumbles in English and sings in tongues after Vodka. Studied at the Ecole des Beaux Arts, Casablanca, Morocco. Presently fulltime author, visual artist in the USA but considers his past irrelevant as he seeks new reincarnations.

LeeAnn Olivier, MFA, is the author of *Doom Loop Wonderland* (The Hunger Press, 2021) and *Spindle, My Spindle* (Hermeneutic Chaos Press, 2016). Her poetry has appeared in *The Missouri Review, Rockvale, Driftwood Press* and elsewhere. Originally from Louisiana, LeeAnn now teaches English at a college in Fort Worth, Texas.

Gregory Ormson lives and writes in Arizona. He was awarded Eastern Iowa Review's lyric narrative prize in 2017 for *Midwest Intimations*. His work has been published in *Quarterly West, Cutbank, The Good Men Project, Unlimited Literature*, and others. Ormson is the author of *Yoga Song* (Rochak Press 2022). https://gregoryormson.com

Quentin Pace is a visual artist, archivist, and librarian working in Houston, TX. He received his BFA and then went on to obtain his Masters of Science in Library Science. He has exhibited at the Lawndale Art Center, the University Museum at Texas Southern, and the Museum of Fine Arts, Houston. In 2019, he held a solo exhibition entitled *Who Is You?* at the Texarkana Regional Arts & Humanities Council (TRAHC). Pace works primarily with acrylic paints, graphite, and pastels.

Robert Palmer is influenced by nature and surroundings. His paintings, more than landscapes physically seen, are an imaginative reflection of feeling on a space remembered. His paintings are reminiscent of the past, capturing a moment in time to preserve a memory. For over twenty years Robert has worked to capture the aesthetic and conceptual mastery of nature. He seeks to tell a story of infinite locations, drawn by the constantly changing celestial light.

Ernst Perdriel is a multifield artist (visual art, photography, writing), designer and horticulturist based in Cowansville (Quebec, Canada). His life's mission is to transmit the passion of the cultural and environmental heritage through arts, lifestyle and sharing of knowledge. He has participated in solo and group exhibitions in visual arts since 1995. His works appeared in *Blue Mesa Review, pacificREVIEW, filling Station, pulpMAG, Sunspot Literary Journal, Meat for Tea, Kolaj, Into the Void*, and others. Learn more at www.ernstperdriel.com.

Ron Pullins is a fiction writer, playwright, and poet working in Tucson AZ. His works in fiction, poetry and drama have been published in numerous journals including *Typishly, Southwest Review, Shenandoah.* A list can be found at www.pullins.com. Pullins won the 2022 Malcolm Lowry award for *Dollartorium*, a satirical novel forthcoming 2023 from J. New Books.

Xiaoqiu Qiu is a Chinese poet who currently is a Black Mountain Institute PhD Fellow at UNLV, a fellowship that counts among its alumni Vu Tran and Alissa Nutting. Qiu writes and translates novels, short stories and poems. His novel *The Man with a Camera Eye* is a semifinalist for the 2021 Autumn House fiction prize. Qiu's poems have been published in *Ghost City Review*, *REED* magazine and *Beyond Words Literary Magazine*, and his translated poems have been published in *Antonym*, *Lunch Ticket*.

Reema Rajbanshi is a published author of creative and critical work, and identifies as South Asian American with Bahujan and Indigenous heritage. Her debut fiction book *Sugar, Smoke, Song* (Red Hen Press, 2020) is a linked story collection exploring the experiences of Asian/American women and immigrant life in the US. Excerpts were published in *Chicago Quarterly Review*, *Confrontation*, *Southwest Review*, and *Blackbird,* among others. Rajbanshi is also a scholar of Literature and has a recent film essay published in *Routledge* (2022).

Oshoto Rowan is a writer and printmaker living in the Pacific Northwest. She loves rain, things with wings, and photographing tiny snippets of shadow filigreed with light. Her visual art can be found on Instagram under the handle @industrialmasquerade.

Jefferey Samoray is based in the metropolitan Detroit area. He earned an MA in English Literature from Binghamton University. After years of working as a marketing writer, Jeff is leveraging his language studies by translating French and Russian poetry. He is also the winner of the French Institute of Michigan's 2021 Fiction Writing Contest (adult category).

Bill Schulz is a Maine-based poet, editor, and artist. He received a Master's in English from the poetry workshop at The University of New Hampshire and a Master's in Theological Studies from The Franciscan School of Theology in Berkeley, California. His work has appeared in *The Aurorean*, *High Shelf*, *Nine Mile*, *Nixes Mate*, *The Seneca Review*, and *Sunspot*. His book of poetry, *Dog or Wolf*, was published in July 2022. He is the founder and editor of *Hole In The Head Review*, www.holeintheheadreview.com.

Born and raised in the busting city of Bangkok, **Penny Senanarong** spends her free time creating and consuming art, whether it be pieces of writing or multimedia works of photography and painting. She has an avid love for the occult and esoteric, as well as for the eldritch and monstrous. Her poetry and short stories can be found at *50-Word Stories*, *Better Than Starbucks*, *Burnt Pine* and *Exeter Enigma*.

Raïssa Simone is a multidisciplinary artist and writer. She has competed at national poetry slams and performed at venues and festivals. Simone has remained active in social justice causes throughout her career, particularly in working to support others living with C-PTSD. She vigorously fights against domestic violence and sexual assault, and centers healing in her poetry.

Dave Sims makes art and music in the mountains of central Pennsylvania. His paintings, comix, stories and poems appear in dozens of tactile and virtual exhibits and publications, with a recent series of five paintings entitled *Survivors* lurking in the virtual pages of the Summer 2023 issue of *Hole in the Head.* A grandfather of several beautiful children, he's also the primary companion to a three-footed jazz turtle named Turk. www.tincansims.com

Valerie A. Smith's first book of poems, *Back to Alabama*, is forthcoming from Sundress Publications. She has a PhD from Georgia State University and an MA from Kennesaw State University, where she currently teaches English. Her poems appear in *Radix, Aunt Chloe, Weber, Spectrum, Obsidian, Crosswinds, Dogwood, Solstice, Oyster River Pages*, and *Wayne Literary Review.* Above all, she values spending quality time with her family.

Leila Batatian Springer has written two novel manuscripts, dabbles in poetry, and won First Prize from *The Writer* for her short story "Hunger." She has given birth twice without anesthesia and found that less painful than trying to get a literary agent.

Christopher Squier is an artist, writer, and cofounder of the art collective Dissolve. His artwork explores optics and the role of light in contemporary visual culture, while his writing addresses research-based projects in a global arts context. He's based in New York City. squier.co

george l stein is a photographer from northern new jersey engaged in street, art, rural and urban decay, alt/portrait and surreal genres. He has previously been published in *Wrongdoing, Fatal Flaw*, and *Sunspot Lit*, among others. Online; georgelstein.com.

Danielle Stonehirsch lives in Maryland and works for Health Volunteers Overseas, a nonprofit focused on global health. Her fiction, poetry, and essays have appeared on the *Tin House* website and in *Bethesda Magazine, Washington City Paper*, and *Montgomery Magazine* as well as various anthologies. She hopes to publish her first novel soon.

Brendan Straubel lives in rural Michigan. His work has appeared in *Dunes, Big Muddy, Michigan-Out-Of-Doors*, and elsewhere. He is a graduate of the University of Missouri-Columbia, where he studied creative writing, journalism, and education.

Santa Cruz poet laureate **David Allen Sullivan**'s books include: *Strong-Armed Angels, Every Seed of the Pomegranate, Bombs Have Not Breakfasted Yet*, and *Black Ice.* He won the Mary Ballard Chapbook poetry prize for *Take Wing*, and *Black Butterflies Over Baghdad* for the Hilary Tham capital collection, Word Works Books.

Ezra Sun is from an amalgamation between New York, Vancouver, and Shanghai. Outside of writing, he enjoys playing the electric guitar, watching Netflix, and solving Sudoku puzzles. He is currently studying physics at the University of Pennsylvania.

Kay Suz is a science fiction writer living in Knoxville, Tennessee. She has a passion for images and words and enjoys putting the two together in any format. She has led writing workshops focusing on short stories, novels, screenplays, and stageplays. She has also directed plays for Underground Stage Company.

C. Tai Tai is an immigrant artist with roots in various parts of the US, Taiwan, and Latin America. Negotiating freedom in self-expression with the fragility of belonging are key themes in her work.

Matina Vossou is a self-taught artist living in Athens, Greece. She uses acrylics and a toothpick, a technique she learned from her father, who was a naïve painter. She paints faces like perfectly unfinished mosaics of emotions and ideas. Vossou believes that every face is a journey. Looking at them is probably going to be our longest, most adventurous and knowledgeable trip.

Suzannah Watchorn is an English-Irish writer who grew up outside of London, UK. She now lives in the United States, where she works as a writing coach and freelance editor. Her current project is a hybrid collection about selves, identity, intimacy, dreams, and imagination.

Rex Wilder is a visual artist and poet living in Benedict Canyon, California. His latest book, *A Quiet Place to Land*, combining images and verbal reflections on a path towards healing from mental illness, is forthcoming from Chatwin Press in Seattle.

Ginna Wilkerson is a poet, artist, and former educator with a Ph.D. in English. She lives in Lexington, KY with her two cats, Amanda and McLain.

Jeanne Wilkinson is an artist and writer who shares time between Brooklyn, NY, and Madison, WI. Her work has been exhibited extensively in galleries worldwide. Her writing and artwork have been featured on NPR's Leonard Lopate Show and Living on Earth, in *Adirondack Review, Columbia Journal Online, J. Mane Gallery, New Millennium Writings, Sunspot Lit,* and more. Her experimental videos have been screened at BAM, at the Greenpoint and New York Independent Film Festivals, and a video installation was featured in a play at the 13th Street Repertory Theater in Manhattan.

William Lewis Winston lives in Oakland, California. His poems appear in *Bearing Witness* (Zephyr Press 2002), *Margie, Ink Pot, Comstock, Poet Lore, Close Up* (Orchard Lea Press 2022), *What Is All This Sweet Work?* (Vita Brevis Press Anthology IV 2022),

Sunspot, and *Consequence*. He received an International Merit Award from *Atlanta Review*. He has processed his own photographs since the age of ten, and until recently, kept the street photography shot in distant lands to himself.

Sheree Wood is a contemporary painter with studios in Milwaukee, WI and Tucson, AZ. From small nature-inspired watercolors to large acrylic abstract paintings, Wood's practice explores color and the way nature affects the human spirit. Wood attributes her manner of seeing the world to a childhood spent camping in the family's red VW bus. Learn more at www.ShereeWoodArt.com.

Ryker Woodward is an oil painter currently located in Monterey, CA. He is known as an abstract expressionist painter who emphasizes experimentation in mediums and compositions. Ryker's current body of work translates video game iconography into a fine art context. Ryker's work has been featured in student shows at Pacific Northwest College of Art in Portland OR where he graduated with a BFA in Painting in 2022.

Helen Wu is a poet who resides in Los Angeles, CA.

Yance Wyatt is a hearing-impaired southerner. He left his home state of Tennessee to study writing at the University of Southern California before serving as their writing center director and writing program professor. A two-time Pushcart Prize nominee, his work has appeared in numerous literary journals including *Zyzzyva* and *Los Angeles Review*. He now lives in Pasadena with his partner, his son, and his eighteen-year-old dog.

Cynthia Yatchman is a Seattle-based artist and art instructor with a BFA in painting (UW). She works primarily on paintings, prints and collages. Her art is housed in numerous public and private collections. She has exhibited on both coasts, extensively in the Northwest, including shows at Seattle University, SPU, Shoreline Community College, the Tacoma and Seattle Convention Centers and the Pacific Science Center. She is a member of the Seattle Print Art Association and COCA-Center of Contemporary Art.

Writing a New World

Sunspot Literary Journal believes in the power of the written word. Fiction, nonfiction, poetry and art can speak truth to power with the power inherent in all human beings. Our mission is to amplify every voice. Four digital quarterly editions are produced per year, along with one print volume.

Support Sunspot Lit

Today more than ever, literary journals are forces of change in the world. *Sunspot Lit* is funded entirely through private means. Every donation, even ones as small as a dollar, makes a difference. Please take a moment to drop a few bucks into the *Sunspot* magnetic field flux.

A PayPal link on the website makes it easy to send a tip, donate enough to publish the next digital edition, or go supernova and fund the next print edition. Please visit https://sunspotlit.com/support for details.

Advertise in *Sunspot*

Classified ads are available in quarterly digital editions and special editions. Spread the word about your writing and arts contests, residency programs, awards, workshops, and more. All classified ads are also posted on the website's classified page. Ad rate: $150 for up to 25 words; $5 for each additional word.

Print ads are available for the annual edition. All ads are black and white. A full page is $850, a half page is $450, and a quarter page is $295. Buy two ads of the same size for the same issue or for two sequential issues to receive a 10% discount. Set up three or more ads and receive a 15% discount.

Sunspot's groovy graphic designer can set up your ad to your specifications. Flat rate of $325, and the design is yours to use multiple times in *Sunspot* or any other magazine.

SUNSPOT LITERARY JOURNAL

WRITING A NEW WORLD

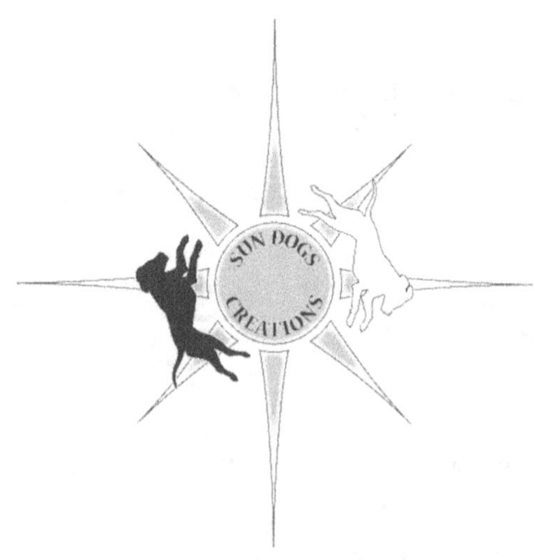

SUN DOGS CREATIONS

CHANGING THE WORLD ONE BOOK AT A TIME

www.ingramcontent.com/pod-product-compliance
Lightning Source LLC
Chambersburg PA
CBHW070445200726
48293CB00007B/2122

* 9 7 8 1 9 5 1 3 8 9 3 5 2 *